Cor

I'll never forget my doctor's bottom-line advice: "You need to reduce your stress level." It sounded great, but how? Here's where my friend Lee Hotchkiss's tool chest of life lessons has offered practical help. If you want to understand and manage stress well, especially in the relational arena, *Stress and Relational Peace* is the book for you. It's great for small group interaction, too.

–Steve Richardson
President, Pioneers USA

Stress and Relational Peace provides a comprehensive and pragmatic set of biblical principles that God intends us to utilize as we develop our character and increase our relational peace to the glory of God.

–Steve Horsman
Alaska Field Director, InterAct Ministries

While serving as a missionary member-care provider in Asia I used and gave away quite a few copies of the little book *Handling Stress Effectively.* What *peace it brought to my life and many other missionaries.* I look forward to reading this updated and expanded edition.

–Dan D.

Stress is what we feel, peace is what we crave. Distilling a lifetime of learning and experience into this book, Hotchkiss offers wise, biblical guidance in the pursuit of peace. His approach has been very helpful for me. Stress is warring against the Church. The "relational peace" emphasis, when applied, really does work!

–Pastor Dave Wiersbe

As a building contractor and Christian of thirty plus years my thirst for tools and knowledge has always continued to grow…and from my first exposure I was hooked…it has helped further my walk and pursuit of the Lord. This recommendation is coming from just another face in the crowd, one of the many in the sea of souls who are pursuing a life with Jesus Christ. If you want to gather more tools to grow in Christ, I recommend that you read this book.You will be blessed!

–Dale L.

ISBN 979-8-89372-384-7

Cover Design by Bari Krisinger
Editorial Assistance by Marcia Zimmermann

Stress and Relational Peace

Marking the Trail for Walking in Peace

Lee Hotchkiss

Stress And Relational Peace

Lee Hotchkiss

Introduction

It has been fifteen years since I wrote the little book, *Handling Stress Effectively: Keeping God at the Center of Life*. It was a small simple book published in 2007 by OM Authentic Books in India and written with an Asian reader in mind. It was based on material that I had taught at that time for 30 years. Ten of those years were working to train missionaries with a large faith mission that worked in 35 countries. The research at that time showed that the number one problem that plagued missionaries was relational difficulties. My own experience as a young missionary had already proved that reality to me personally. There was something about the stresses of cross-cultural ministry that caused dedicated people undue difficulty in their relationships. Much of this current book comes from both my missionary and pastoral experience and my work trying to understand that dynamic and provide biblical solutions.

My objective in writing *Handling Stress Effectively* was to equip pastors and lay-workers around the world with ministry skills to help others who were experiencing stress. There appeared to be a need for providing tools for those working in pastoral ministry in the rapidly growing church in Asia. The English version of that little book has been reprinted several times and published in five additional languages. Wherever I spoke about stress I found genuine interest. I have taught on this subject in approximately 50 countries and discovered that people readily identified with experiencing stress and were eager to explore practical solutions from a biblical perspective. Stress transcends cultures, ethnic and national boundaries.

It has been my intent for some time to update and expand that first book and explore more fully the connection between stress and relational peace. I have reorganized and added new material that I think is needed for today. Currently the world is experiencing a period of high stress caused by the COVID-19 pandemic, heightened political division, war, plus ominous predictions of drought, famine and economic collapse. The news is filled with clear evidence of an uptick in a wide range of stress reactions. There are street protests, a rise in violence, physical and sexual abuse, a heightened volume and intensity of expressions of anger, public use of vulgar memes and gestures, political division, drug and alcohol abuse, suicide, homicide and broken relationships. This should not surprise us as the Bible tells us this will happen in the "last days" (1Timothy 4:1-2; 2 Timothy 3:1-5). Christians need to be equipped to deal with their own stress during these turbulent times but also ready to minister to others. I am motivated to act now as the opportunity for the Church to have relevant ministry has never been greater. The challenge for the Church is to equip believers who are living under the mounting perils of stress in a rapidly dystopian world. A practical theology of stress from a biblical perspective is needed now more than ever.

This, of course, needs to start in the family. Kids feel stress but rarely know how to cope so they act out in ways that can be destructive. Parents need to model and actively teach their children the principles you will find in this book. Conflict in churches and ministry teams are also arenas where a biblical understanding and application of stress management is desperately needed. My challenge to you is simple: Read, Digest and Share. Discuss the concepts found in each chapter with someone. Form an accountability partnership or small group for the purpose of taking steps of personal application. Ask for accountability. Ask God to open doors to share these truths with others. Life-changing learning works best when Jesus is in charge and when we work together with others under His leadership. Put Him in charge of the process.

My desire is to share with you the best that I have learned over my years of ministry in a style that is personal and practical. I realize that I have entered that phase of life when my task is to focus on passing the best lessons to the next generation. There are plenty of academic papers and books on different aspects of stress and relationships, thus I will endeavor to communicate in plain language. I have been cautioned to not get too deep into the weeds by citing academic and research studies. The advice was simple and to the point. People are interested in what helps them cope. That advice keeps ringing in my ears as I try to sort and summarize my thoughts on this massive subject. I continue to read research, but I don't want to get get bogged down by trying to be too academic or overly detailed. My objective is to be practical, biblical and focus on application. Linking stress and relationship, however, is complex and I will do my best to summarize and stick to the most important things. Most of all I want to point you to "Jesus, the author and perfecter of our faith" (Hebrews 12:2, 12-14). Join me as I share from my life-long study and pursuit to keep God at the center of life. I have not arrived, nor do I have all the answers, but God has been graciously at work in my journey as I continue to learn to manage my stress more effectively and to live in relational peace. My best advice is simply, keep your eyes on Jesus. In Chapter 1 I will lay the groundwork for an overall plan to identify where stress originates and how it contaminates and spreads to various areas of life. I will also introduce a strategy for getting started (Identify – Act – Rest). I will present several simple memory hooks to aid in remembering key concepts. I find that this helps me recall and apply truth to my own life and helps communicate these truths to others. People don't carry around reference books but mental images and memory hooks are a practical way to help remember when you need to apply the concepts in real life situations.

Chapter 2 will focus on the personal emotional aspect of stress reactions and how they are linked to the ways that you process disappointment. I will present a model to help you build an action plan that will make a difference in daily life.

In Chapter 3 I will tackle the connection between stress and personal identity. I will show where you can find worth and value apart from an accomplishment and performance model.

Section II, Chapters 4 through 9 will pivot from personal peace to relational peace. I will explore how they are connected and influence each other. I will examine six key disciplines that can both transform relationships and protect you from the negative effects of stress.

In Section III, Chapters 10 through 14 will return to the big picture and focus on five practical activities to help build a life of healthy discipline that undergirds relationships of peace. In Chapter 14 I will briefly touch on the physiological aspect of stress and suggest some practical strategies that you can take.

In Section IV I have added some illustrative stories from the lives of biblical characters and people from the present day that you can learn from as you observe both positive and negative responses to stress.

The Addendum will provide supplemental information that may be helpful but didn't seem to fit well, so I tacked it on at the end for your reference.

Let's get started.

Section I

The Personal Side of Stress
Foundational Principles

Chapter 1

Getting Started – A Map Through The Forest

Every journey has a starting point. Plotting a journey with a GPS (Global Positioning System) begins by identifying your current location. It then asks where you want to end up. Keeping the end in view is a good principle for life. The Bible puts a high priority on living in relational peace. The path for getting there can, at times, seem like you are lost in the forest. I want to provide you with a map for understanding the relationship between stress and relational peace. I want to help you develop a plan as to how you can proceed toward the desired destination of living in relational peace. Before getting started with developing an action plan, there are some basic concepts that will help clarify the big picture. Let's begin with some of these background facts about stress. These three big ideas about stress will help you understand the terrain that you are traversing. There are three vital things you need to know about stress.

Stress is about Control

The first big idea is that the term stress refers to your personal reactions to any event which you cannot control. These are called stressors. I will use the word "event" to keep it simple. These events can be past, present or future. They can be real or imagined. The key is to realize that you react to events that are not in your control or that you believe are beyond your power to change. Human beings share the fantasy that, if they could control everything, then life would be better, more ideal and less stressful. This goes all the way back to the Garden of Eden and the Fall. The serpent tempted Eve with the idea of becoming "like God" (Genesis 3:5). Ever since, mankind has been striving to functionally supplant God and be in control. At the core is the common belief that life would be better if you were in control of everything. Stress reactions are a symptom and result of this fundamental misbelief that all share: that you should be able to control everything in your life.

It is true that God has given man responsibility to make choices and control some things. God delegated to Adam a significant "dominion role" in the garden "to cultivate it and keep it" (Genesis 1:28; 2:15). Leadership and management are examples of this principle. These important roles need to be exercised under God's leadership or they can generate a good deal of stress and relational problems. Much suffering can be traced back to people trying to dominate and exert control over others (more on this subject later). Stress can also be caused by a function of failing to take action act when you should. At other times it comes from taking action that you shouldn't. Many of the things that cause stress are of our own making. That was certainly true of Adam, Eve and their son Cain. Bad choices can have long and severe consequences.

A generally accepted definition of stress is reaction to what you cannot control. If you can control the event in question, then you probably should take a problem-solving approach. I will include a sample problem solving strategy in the addendum at the end of the book. Part of clarifying a stress event is asking the questions: "Is there any action you can take to change the situation? What power or control do you have that would make a difference in changing this situation?" The way you answer these questions can direct you to take a problem-solving approach. Ask God to guide you to take wise action steps and then rest in His leading (Psalm 32:8; 37:23). Stress, however, by definition is not having control.

Stress is Variable

The second big idea is that stress is variable. It can be either good or bad. It can push you to higher performance or it can paralyze and defeat you. It can be chronic or acute, that is to say, it can last a long time or be only for a short duration. Another variable is intensity. The cause can be traumatic or be generated from a seemingly inconsequential irritant. It can also be external or internal. This means it can come from an outside (exogenous) circumstance in your world or it can come from inside you (endogenous). Stress can also be cumulative. That means it can have carryover from a previous event or from a series of events that continue to trigger leftover feeling. Fear and anxiety are examples of this process. These can develop into habits that you carry from one event to the next. When not processed well they can exacerbate the cumulative effects of stress. This can explain why sometimes a person will explode with a reaction that seems way out of proportion from a small triggering event.

Understanding this can help you make sense of what is being called traumatic stress syndrome.

Stress is About Interpreting Events

The **third big idea** about stress is the way an event is interpreted or processed will greatly influence the intensity of your stress reactions. A good way to clarify this is to ask, "What significance are you attaching to this event?" Or, "How does this event correspond to your expectations of how things should be - your ideal?" In a perfect world all the events of your life would match your values, ideals and expectations. Stress reactions are generated when you realize that you are not able to control the details of your world. We are back to that first big idea about stress. It really is all about control.

The Importance of Having a Plan and Taking Strategic First Steps

Having a plan can provide hope. Before we get too involved with the complexity of stress reactions, let's summarize how you can get started. A simple three-step model is useful. I call it the **Identify – Act – Rest** model. This approach can provide you with a starting point for diminishing your stress reactions.

Start with **Identify**. Ask, "If I were God for just five minutes what would I change?" This is a great way to quickly identify the event that is generating your stress reactions. Ask God to help you identify what the real issue is (Psalm 139:1-4, 23; Jeremiah 17:9-10). You may also ask a friend to help. Most of us are masters of self-deception and we can go to great lengths to avoid the real issues. Often it is important to recognize that the actions of others are a common source of irritation and frustration. One of the most dangerous misbeliefs that we harbor is that we can control other people's behavior.

Next, assess what **Action** is appropriate. For a believer, prayer should always be the first action we take. From the beginning to the end the Bible places a great deal of emphasis on the importance of prayer. The first and most important action is to bring the matter to God in prayer. This can take various forms. It can be a quick cry for help or a request for God to intervene in the event itself (Philippians 4:6). An important word of caution; you should not view prayer as an attempt to control God. He is not like the genie from Aladdin's lamp that grants you three wishes. Prayer needs to be exercised in a spirit of submission to God. Your first priority is to acknowledge that you live under God's sovereignty and providence in all things. You can do this on a daily basis as you pray about specific events before they happen, as they unfold and after they occur. It is the before, during and after sort of praying where you can encircle or bathe the event in prayer. Following this action step (which may be more of a season of prayer) you can move toward cultivating your rest in Jesus' control of all things and His good purpose for you (Psalm 138:8; Romans 8:28-29). During this activity some additional action steps may begin to clarify.

Rest in Jesus. This rest needs to be nurtured. It grows as we trust Him. It comes by faith as you feed your mind and soul on the Word of God. His Word will remind you again and again that God is in control. He has promised to bring good out of any and all situations (Romans 8:28). You can learn to rejoice and rest in Him no matter how much stress you are experiencing at the moment. Developing a personal practical theology of rest is a powerful weapon for combating stress (Psalm 37:7; Isaiah 40:31; Matthew 11:28-30).

A useful memory hook that I will use throughout this book is Head – Heart – Hands. I have used this model when teaching groups that are less tied to taking notes with pencil and paper. I recall speaking at a conference of Christian workers where ten different languages were spoken. These men were dedicated and smart, but I realized that I needed to make the concepts easy for them to remember and communicate. This also helps visual learners, like me, who need to see something visual to help remember and use when dealing with abstract concepts.

Use Your Head

You identify things with your **Head.** You perceive your world with your **Head.** God has created the head with eyes, ears and a brain. This is how you investigate, take in information and process data from your surrounding world. Jesus had a lot to say about the importance of the eye. "The eye is the lamp of the body; so then if your eye is clear, your whole body will be full of light. But if your eye is bad, your whole body will be full of darkness. If then the light that is in you is darkness, how great is the darkness" (Matthew 6:22-23)! He then went on to speak about the importance of keeping your eye gate clean in order to have effective ministry with others (Matthew 7:3-5). Identifying patterns of human behavior is an important part of trying to make sense of the events that are happening. The bottom line is - use your head to identify,

Tend Your Heart

The **Heart** is the center or core of the person. The word *heart* is used in the Bible in several ways. Occasionally it speaks of the physical organ that pumps the blood, but usually it is used as a metaphor. It often refers to the whole person but can also speak of one or more aspects of the soul. A good definition of the soul is the capacity to think, feel and choose (that sounds a lot like the Head – Heart – Hands model). The believer in Jesus must remember that the inner person of the heart demands careful oversight and diligent attention (Proverbs 4:23). We process information with our head and our heart. The Bible often uses the terms head and heart interchangeably and each can speak of the "inner person" or non-material aspect of the person. Context is paramount when doing Bible study well.

In this book I will usually refer to the heart as the center of emotions. There is a risk of pushing this model too far, but generally it is helpful to distinguish between thinking and feelings. The heart is positioned between the head and the hands. There is an obvious connection. You are a whole person. But as with the physical body there is coordination. The members of your body work together. There is interaction and each member exerts influence on the other members. What you think will change what you do. I have found this a very helpful construct and easy to remember and teach. People are quick to grasp the idea of head, heart, and hands – the capacity to think, feel and do. Many people are unaware of how strategic and powerful the interaction is within these members. Each capacity can clearly influence the other two. It is easy to underestimate the important role each play in a person's life. Each requires a biblical management plan to live a God-centered healthy life.

Hands to the Work

In this model the **Hands** represent taking action. In the Bible the hand often speaks of power. Your hands can remind you that you are empowered (when yielded to the Holy Spirit) to respond to the truth you discover with your head (Romans 6:8-14). Your hands can remind you of the importance of acting and not just exploring ideas or getting stuck in ruminating on negative thoughts. Jesus was very clear that obedience to truth is the way of wisdom (Matthew 7:24-27). Putting truth into action is an important strategy.

Stress can trigger a spiritual battle that involves the whole person including the head, heart, and hands. In a battle there is a time to do reconnaissance (identify) and to strategize. There is a time to take action and a time to rest.

When something bad happens, our enemy, the devil, tries to defeat us by undermining our belief in God's integrity. He will whisper, "Is God credible? He is not all-powerful and certainly not loving. A loving powerful God would not allow this to happen. See, God is not trustworthy and therefore not worthy of your trust. You are on your own here." Satan always tries to undermine God's character and attack your ability to trust and rest in Him. Satan seems to be especially active when we are under stress and things are not going according to our expectations. Satan knows that believers are particularly vulnerable to temptation at these times. This is the arena where real spiritual battles take place. Two key questions are: "Is God good?" And "Is He in control?" These are watershed questions. How we answer these questions is at the heart of every battle. It also serves as a foundational starting point in understanding stress for the believer. There are, however, a myriad of other important conclusions you need to monitor and manage in order to stay healthy when things go wrong.

Stress is About Sovereignty

Stress is about control and therefore it is about sovereignty. A very important lesson in the Bible is the testimony of King Nebuchadnezzar, possibly the most powerful king in all human history. This is the story of how God humbled him for seven years and then restored him to his position of power and rule. It appears that God, through Daniel, is making a big statement about the limits God places upon world leaders and human empires. Nebuchadnezzar the King of Babylon is pictured as the head of gold. God taught him about his limits of sovereignty and dominion. In studying this chapter you will notice that the phrase "Most High God" is used six times (repeated for emphasis) and speaks of the fact that He alone is the sovereign ruler over the realm of mankind and bestows dominion to whomever He wishes (Daniel 4:2-3, 17, 25-26, 32, 34, 37). This truth that God is sovereign is clearly stated in Scripture (Psalm 93:1-2; 96:10; 97:1; 99:1 and 1 Timothy 6:15). The big application question for every believer is, "Why are we so slow to apply this truth to everyday events that we don't like?"

Rolling Stress Onto God

It is interesting that the Hebrew word for *commit* is the word *"roll."* In the book of Joshua the story is told of God preparing the Israelites to enter the Promised Land. It tells us that the Lord "rolled away the reproach" of their experience of slavery in Egypt. That place was called Gilgal: the place of rolling. This is a great picture of how to deal with stress.

"Now when Joshua was near Jericho he looked up and saw a man standing in front of him with a drawn sword in his hand. Joshua went up to him and asked, 'Are you for us or for our enemies?' 'Neither,' he replied, 'but as commander of the army of the LORD I have now come.' Then Joshua fell facedown to the ground in reverence, and asked him, 'What message does my LORD have for his servant.?' The commander of the LORD's army replied, 'Take off your sandals, for the place where you are standing is holy.' And Joshua did so" (Joshua 5:13-15).

Just as Joshua, the leader of Israel, was called to acknowledge God's sovereignty by bowing in worship, we are called to do the same. Joshua was called to be a leader under God's authority, not to rule as a king. You and I are likewise called to be servant-leaders, not kings. Kings are sovereign, they control things. You and I are called to acknowledge God's sovereignty in every circumstance and in every situation. Worship is at the core of a godly life. It is bowing to acknowledge who God is – that He alone is the Sovereign King. Living in this reality defeats much of stress's punch.

In practice, this acknowledgment requires us to bow in worship and in recognition of God's sovereignty. This needs to be an ongoing activity as life happens day by day and moment by moment. You can either react in the flesh or you can respond in the Spirit. As the old saying goes, "Stress will make you either bitter or better." This commitment to bow in worship will be tested time and time again as the events of life unfold.

King David said it clearly; "Commit your way to the LORD" (Psalm 37:5). We could paraphrase this verse and say, "Roll onto the Lord the leadership to set the direction for your path forward." When you choose to take the ultimate responsibility for establishing your own path things can get really messed up. King Saul's life is a tragic example. God has not designed you to carry this heavy load of life, ministry and leadership alone. The Hebrew word for commit (roll) as we saw in Joshua Chapter 5 is the action step that is an important starting point.

Another example of this concept was written by Solomon, "Commit to the LORD whatever you do, and your plans will succeed" (Proverbs 16:3). This is not a magic formula to guarantee success for whatever you want to do, but rather it speaks of rolling onto the Lord the leadership of the details in all things. It is asking the Sovereign Lord to be in charge of specific life events and letting Him bring blessing as He sees fit. "Trust in the LORD with all your heart and lean not on your own understanding; in all your ways acknowledge him, and he will make your paths straight" (Proverbs 3:5-6).

God is seeking those who will trust Him with a whole heart and follow Him through any and every circumstance, not turning aside to their own understanding but acknowledging Him as Lord in every new event. Roll onto the Lord the weight of any burden that comes as you acknowledge His role as the Sovereign One of your life. This is an action step of faith represented by your hands. It is something you do. The Holy Spirit will produce fruit in your heart that includes the emotions of love, joy, and peace. His fruit produces rest (Galatians 5:22-23).

Learning to Rest

The Bible repeatedly instructs the believer to rest. This heart function requires cooperation from the head and the hands. "Rest in the Lord and wait patiently for Him; Do not fret..." (Psalm 37:7). The "faith-rest" theme is developed in Hebrews 3:11-4:19. The writer appears to include both the rest that God offers in salvation (realizing salvation is not works-based) and His rest offered in the sanctification process as we grow in Christ. They each call for the action of faith and lead us to rest in Christ. Your soul can rest by faith in the promise that God will finish what He has started (Philippians 1:6). This is why it is called the faith-rest principle. Believing in God's promises is the pathway to learning God's soul rest.

Stress is Complex

Another significant idea concerning stress is that it can become incredibly complicated. Using systems theory can help simplify this complexity. When action is taken early in the cycle it can also lessen the range of damage it might normally take. Prompt action pays off. Identify repeating patterns early and take action. This can get you back on track. Paring systems theory with Scripture can be a powerful approach. The principles from God's Word will shine light on your path and give clarity for your next steps (Psalm 119:105). The Stress Cycle is a descriptive model but it can lead you to God's Word which is prescriptive.

The first big idea in systems theory is that *everything in a system affects everything else in the system*. Systems theory is used in many disciplines of study today such as engineering, management, ecology, biology and medicine. I have been using a systems approach to better understand stress and how it influences human behavior for the past 45 years. I have found that charting stress reactions with a visual aid helps me. I can better visualize how these stress reactions develop and where they will likely go next. The stress pathway is often disruptive and sometimes even destructive like a tornado that skips across the ground. The Stress Cycle helps identify where best to take action.

The second significant idea taken from systems theory is that it is useful to find *"leverage points"* or places to best intervene in the system to bring about the most change in the whole of the system. I have already shared one of the most important points of intervention – that is to commit an event to God in prayer. Subsequent chapters will deal with additional points of intervention around the Stress Cycle

The Stress Cycle illustrates how one area of my life is interconnected with other areas. Developing the habit of thinking before acting is an important safeguard. The discipline of taking time to walk around the stress cycle and to explore and identify your personal habits at each point is powerful. It is good to see not only what is going on in each area but also how each area is being influenced, as well as exerting pressure on every other area around the cycle. Remember in systems theory everything affects everything else.

It is one thing to see the theory of how things connect, but when stress flares up your stress reactions can blindside you before you spot them. When a negative event happens (as identified at the top of the model) it can trigger a rapid chain reaction that quickly occurs around the entire cycle. It is easy to lose perspective and do or say something that you might not under normal circumstances. Acute stress can even produce a kind of brain fog that is disorienting and makes it difficult to think clearly. We can react out of habit without thinking about the consequences. Quick words and actions can do a lot of damage. James' strategic teaching on the use of the tongue is a good reminder (James 1:19-20, 3:1-12). It can be a real safeguard to have a trusted person to consult with before acting. There is safety in having a wise sounding board (Proverbs 11:14).

Identifying common pathways around the Stress Cycle is a wise starting place for insightful change. Spotting connections and how quickly they progress can be very helpful. Each person is unique. Everyone will have distinctive strengths, weaknesses, and habits in how they react. Remember that these habit patterns usually run deep and can be stubborn and persistent. We all have blind spots. Stress reactions can be triggered without much regard for the consequences. Unfinished business at any point around the Stress Cycle tends to intensify all the other stress reactions.

Models like the Stress Cycle can help us grow in becoming more Christ- like.

You can start at any point on the cycle and begin to ask:

1) What is going on here?

2) What are the dynamics?

3) Are there any patterns that are repeating?

4) How is this area affecting other areas of my life?

5) How are other areas of the cycle affecting this area?

6) How is the stress that I am experiencing pushing me to react?

These and similar questions are helpful in applying the Identify – Act – Rest model.

"Stories That Illustrate" (Section IV) can help you practice spotting stress patterns in other people's stories and possible action steps they could have taken. As you read, you may discover things that seem obvious from an outside perspective. Remember that during an experience everything may seem very confusing, frustrating, and disconnected and even hopeless. You can learn as you observe others. Develop your skill by identifying patterns in the stories. Remember everything in the Stress Cycle affects everything else in the cycle. Ask God to help you learn and grow in your ability to identify and discern how your reactions are related and connected.

Perceptions

The arrow at the top right of the Stress Cycle represents your Perceptions and Thoughts as you process an event. This is probably the most important dynamic from a mental health perspective. The conclusions that you draw about the events of your life tell a great deal about your mental, emotional, and relational health. Ask God to help you discern what is true and what is not.

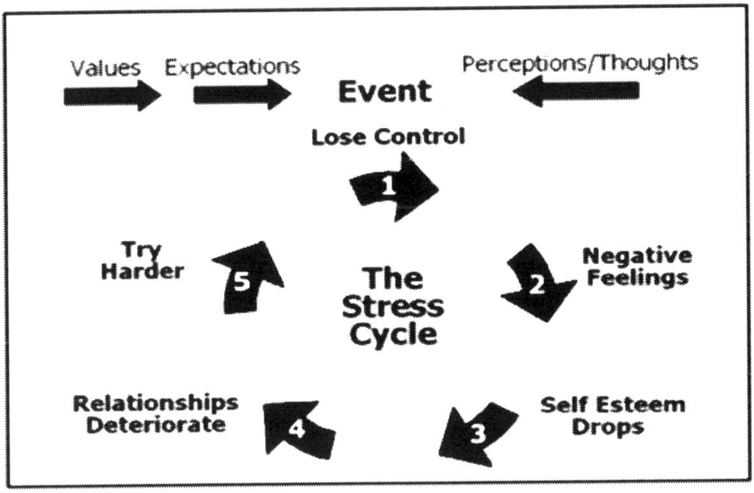

Values and Expectations

The two arrows at the top left side of the Stress Cycle, "Values" and "Expectations", represent what you bring to every event. Clarifying them can help you better understand where your stress originates.

When I provided pre-marital counseling to couples, I would try to facilitate good communication between the individuals regarding what values and expectations they were bringing to the marriage relationship. Often these values would be different from the other person. I would say, "These are the things that will surprise you, possibly even years from now, and if not careful you may be tempted to fight about them." The values that set up your expectations of how things *should be* can run deep. They represent your worldview.

These values can be broken down into four general categories: cultural values, family values, religious values, and personal values. A little exploration here may be useful in dispelling some of the mystery.

Cultural Values: Cultural values are the collectively held customs that nations or people groups have in common. These shared values are the unwritten rules by which a society lives. An example from Japan may help illustrate. The Japanese place a high value on conformity. It is said, "the nail that sticks up gets pounded down." If a student from Japan is in a situation where they are not able to conform to the group, it is probably going to be stressful. This discomfort will depend on the student's personal application of this collective cultural value to their own life and expectations. The student's own stress level will be determined by how important they perceive this value to be in the particular event. Their stress reactions may vary depending on their own sense of well-being, confidence or insecurity, and a host of other factors; but cultural values will play a big part in their individual stress response.

Family Values: Family values somewhat overlap with cultural values. In some cultures, these "family of origin" values can be even more significant than cultural values. These "family of origin" values are very powerful and long lasting. I am still discovering how the family that I grew up in has shaped me. I was raised in a family where my parents believed in the value of hard work. That family value has often controlled my expectations about how I should work and how I think everyone else around me should work. That, of course, can set me up for stress in the workplace, especially when I have the responsibility to supervise others and assess their performance.

Religious Values: Religious or faith values often run deep and can be very powerful. As a Christian your values should be in the process of becoming more aligned with biblical values. I have a friend who was raised in a very legalistic belief system. As an adult he finds it very difficult not to be legalistic in every part of his life even though he left that faith tradition long ago. What you have been taught from your early religious upbringing, rightly or wrongly, affects your sense of moral code and your expectations.

Personal Values: Personal values are those stable long-term values that you have settled upon and incorporated into your life that may set you apart from others, even when you share the other three value areas with them. These personalized core beliefs make you unique and distinct as an individual.

Your values act as a filter or lens through which you perceive your world. You try to make sense of events as you perceive them through these filters. Deep values produce strong convictions, expectations, and shape the way you process every event. Understanding this will help you see the powerful link between your values, expectations and perceptions at the top of the Stress Cycle. I have observed that the greater the stress I am under the more I tend to gravitate back to my core values to find stability. An action step that I personally find helpful for managing my stress is to pray that Jesus Christ will be Lord over my values, expectations and perceptions. My ongoing prayer is that He will shape and mold all three so that they are pleasing to Him (Ephesians 5:10).

Seeing Your Stress

The Stress Cycle helps us become aware of our own stress. Pausing to take inventory of stress reactions allows us to identify and take action. When we fail to do this, we are often confronted by growing discomfort. Our reactions soon become more pronounced by negative emotions, erosion in our sense of identity, relational deterioration and physical tension. Left unattended the downward spiral usually continues. A lot of damage and debris can result that require additional cleanup action. This downward movement can be summed up as a loss of peace and joy. The Stress Cycle is a great tool used by your head to observe and identify so that you can take appropriate action as you seek to enjoy His rest that comes from walking in fellowship with Christ.

Discuss:

1) Identify some values that influence your expectations.

2) Think of a recent event that was stressful to you.

3) What was beyond your control? Was problem-solving appropriate?

4) Are you able to identify and put into words your emotions?

5) What evidence was there that your stress reactions progressed around the Stress Cycle?

6) How can you use the (Identify – Action – Rest) method?

7) How is the (Head - Hands - Heart) memory hook helpful?

Chapter 2

A God-Centered Emotional Life

Society today puts a great deal of emphasis on feelings and emotions. It has been suggested that this current generation (for the past 75 years or so) has elevated the importance of the individual's feelings, possibly as a reaction to those who in earlier times placed prominence on the disciplines of behavior and thinking. Those who try to explain this shift point to the influence of post-modernism which has promoted the individual's experience as the ultimate authority. Thus, you hear statements like, "This is my reality." In hermeneutics (science of interpretation) a shift can clearly be seen away from seeking to determine what the author intended. Now the focus is on the reader. It is common to hear statements like, "To me it means..." As philosophy has lost hope for discovering ultimate truth, the center of attention has shifted to experience. Each person can make up their own truth and reality. This move toward emotions and the individual's right to establish a "personal reality" go together. The emphasis is now on a person's subjective thoughts and feelings as the ultimate bar of authority. The result is an exemption from outside questioning, judgment or accountability. The ultimate offense today in the public square is to offend someone's feelings or to question the authority of their opinion. It is into this arena that we step as we explore this volatile topic.

Defining Terms

A good place to begin any discussion is to clarify definitions. I will use feelings and emotions somewhat interchangeably as does the Merriam-Webster online dictionary. In the counseling world, the word "affect" is commonly used for emotions. The word "dysfunction" is still used when behavior drives emotions that are counterproductive to the functioning of the person. The term "distress" is often used for a more extreme emotional state. In the medical community the physical body is said to be "in distress" when in danger of ceasing to function. It also carries a technical meaning that refers to a negative state of failure to cope with stress (a maladaptive response that diminishes functioning) or to the heightened emotional reaction caused by a stressful event (a stressor).

In the Bible the word *distress* is used broadly in both Old and New Testaments and deserves careful attention. The word *stress* is not found in the Bible as it is a modern word having been coined by Hans Selye, the endocrinologist who introduced the term. The English word *distress* is found only 83 times, but when you search the nearly 20 Greek and Hebrew words associated with it, the use jumps to over 450 times. If the search is expanded to include related words like sorrow or trouble, you discover a vast subject that demands more study (see Addendum for more on this subject).

The biblical writers speak about distress in three general categories; (1) external events that are distressful, often describing people being in circumstances of trouble or "straits" of some kind, (2) the emotional feelings of distress that people experience internally, and (3) the distress caused by God's hand of judgment, sometimes past and sometimes pointing to a future time of great trouble or tribulation that is predicted to come upon the world that will produce great distress upon mankind.

Earlier I presented the foundational concept that most negative feelings are a product of how events are processed. When faced with circumstances that are beyond one's control, a biological pathway of biochemical changes take place that can be measured in the production of stress hormones in the physical body. I will come back to this concept in Chapter 14. For now, I want to focus on how we commonly think about these negative feelings. The average person describes these experiences with words like frustration, guilt, fear, and anger. These common feelings are familiar to us. They are very personal and can be frequent and even overwhelming. Negative feelings can do an amazing amount of damage when mismanaged, left unattended or acted out. As you learn to use the Stress Cycle you will begin to see how poor management of your emotional life can contaminate and complicate your self-concept, relationships, and even your physical health.

Managing and Mismanaging Emotions

There are two simple ways people generally mismanage emotions. I think of managing my emotions much like walking a tightrope. Staying up on the wire requires balance, skill, attention and a lot of practice. Falling off means I need to get back up and learn from my mistake. This is a good mental picture of learning to manage emotions. Falling off one side is what can be called "acting out" feelings. Falling off the other side of the rope would represent suppressing or denying feelings. Someone expressed this as trying to "bury" feelings by pretending that they don't exist. Some people are more prone to lean to one side and some to the other of this emotional tightrope.

Acting out behaviors can be illustrated by an angry person who throws things, shouts, swears, drives aggressively, hits people, slams his fist on the table and walks out of a discussion, engages in sexually immoral behavior, throws temper tantrums, engages in binge eating, or tells off the boss and quits his job, just to name a few. These exaggerated behaviors are designed to let everyone around know that they are unhappy. Like an actress on the stage displaying her emotion, everyone in the audience knows what she is feeling. Acting out draws attention to what is going on inside.

Acting out behaviors can make big messes that can get you into big trouble socially. The legal system in most countries is designed to regulate the worst kinds of acting out behaviors by establishing laws to limit certain conduct. If you act out by striking someone with your fist you may go to jail. It is intended to act as a behavioral deterrent. Society, and most organizations, also try to limit behaviors by establishing rules and using shame or public social pressure to conform individuals to selected norms. But what about the so called permissible, less-offensive kinds of acting out like slamming doors, throwing things, or raising one's voice? Cultural and social norms are dynamic and are currently changing in the direction of permitting more acting out, but there are lines that you had better not cross if you want to stay out of trouble. Everyone practices a range of acting out behaviors, even if only to a moderate degree. These, however, can quickly become unhealthy, self-defeating, damaging to your relationships and not glorifying to God.

Denial behaviors are a way of pretending you don't feel. These may, on the surface, look more spiritual, but when you act as if you do not feel emotions, you are playing a dangerous game of dishonesty. Burying feelings can cause them to "go underground" and it may end up costing you in the long run. Turning emotions inside and pretending that they don't exist is not a healthy habit. Cultures that put an emphasis on face-saving tend to use denial to a greater extent.

In some circumstances holding your tongue can be a good thing (Proverbs 10:19), but a habit of never acknowledging your feelings, or stuffing them down inside can lead to physical illness and inner turmoil.

Most people do some acting out and some stuffing down depending on the situation. In public you may stuff it and at home let it all out. This can cause additional stress by straining relationships within the family. This tends to be more common in face-saving cultures or homes that put a high value on public image.

You may stay out of trouble in one arena but create additional problems in another. You may be able to avoid getting into trouble in public, but you know that your behavior is not glorifying God. You know it; God sees it and it will have a chilling effect on your fellowship with God. There is a better way. Let's explore three healthy, biblical principles to help manage emotions to the glory of God. Note that each of these takes us back to the attributes of God.

Three Biblical Principles for Managing Emotions

To help me remember these principles I use the Head - Heart - Hands memory hook that I introduced earlier. I will explore the use of each to help you manage your emotions. After you identify the feeling, you can begin to take three types of actions. The first action is a *Hands* strategy and it will assist you in moving in the direction of peace and rest.

1. Do What Is Right.

Behavior influences emotions. This first principle is simple but true. What you do affects how you feel. When you do the right thing, you feel better. This is a *hands* strategy. Even when the results are not immediate, over time doing the right thing helps give stability and leads to growing toward emotional maturity. Both acting out and pouting are immature expressions of emotions. They can also be sinful and damaging to your relationships.

Feeling better is a good reason to do what is right, but there is something more fundamental for the Christian. If God has clearly revealed His character to be holy and righteous, if the Bible teaches that it is His will for His children to live out holy and righteous lives that reflect His character, and if God created man to glorify and please Him in all of life, then doing the right thing is no longer a matter primarily about how one feels. It becomes an issue of honor. We honor God when we live in a manner that is consistent with His nature as we reflect what it means to be a member of His family. The center of your focus and motivation begin to shift – it comes down to God's glory.

Doing what is right is about doing righteousness. The Christian is to practice righteousness out of a desire to please God. He wants you to find your greatest joy and pleasure in your relationship with Him.

Understanding the link between behavior and emotions is crucially important. Doing righteousness does influence your emotions. Joy and peace can supplant anxiety and frustration as you live by faith, knowing that God will keep His promises of future blessing. Looking beyond the present circumstance and living in the sure expectation of hope that God will bring good out of each stressful event leads to peace (Romans 8:28).

By faith you can begin to "consider it pure joy" when you face trials as you come to understand the reality of the Scripture that says the testing of your faith develops perseverance. You will begin to realize that this important work that God is doing is His plan for making you to be mature and complete (James 1:2-4). This faith perspective is an important link between emotions and behavior. As you submit to the Holy Spirit, He will empower you to manage this dynamic for God's glory.

There are many specific behaviors that affect emotions; praise and worship are good examples. Focusing the mind on God in worship and opening the mouth to praise Him brings a better perspective to life and changes the emotional climate in the heart. The Apostle Paul put it this way, "Rejoice in the Lord always; again I will say, rejoice" (Philippians 4:4)!

Forgiveness is another behavior that changes emotions. Many people forget that forgiveness is a choice that is made in obedience to God's Word. It is the right thing to do. When a person chooses to hold a grudge and foster feelings of resentment, it continues to weigh upon the emotions and cultivate more guilt. Forgiveness is an act of the will whereby a person releases what has been held against another.

When you do what is right morally, you feel better than when you do anything that you know is morally wrong. Doing what is morally right affects feelings. Guilt is both a judicial standing before God (objective guilt) and a feeling (subjective guilt).

Eating a good diet and living a disciplined life have emotional rewards as well. Getting enough sleep and physical exercise can help modify emotions. Research has shown that aerobic exercise produces neurotransmitters and can actually modify brain chemistry, which in turn can lift minor depression. Right behaviors can change some aspects of physiology. I am not suggesting that exercise will solve all clinical depression, but it is fair to say it is a helpful strategy in mood management.

The practice of self-discipline is becoming a lost art in much of modern society. A whole generation has been raised on the philosophy, "If it feels good, do it." Many marketing jingles echo in our heads that encourage you to follow your feelings. These marketing strategies have sold huge amounts of product, but have also eroded the belief that self-discipline is important for living a godly life.

Self-discipline is about learning to do what is right no matter how loudly the feelings may howl and scream. I am not suggesting that you gut-it-out by disengaging from your emotions. The goal is not to practice some kind of stoic detachment from them. What I am saying is that one of the age-old measures of maturity is not letting your emotions set the agenda for your behavior. Impulse control is an important part of growing into maturity and is much needed today.

This kind of spiritual and emotional maturity comes over time as you submit control of specific events to God. Christ gives the grace and power to do what is right (Philippians 4:13, 2 Peter 1:3-9). Self-control is a fruit of the Holy Spirit (Galatians 5:22-25) and as you walk in step with Him, under His influence and control, He grows this wonderful spiritual fruit in your life.

We clearly see the importance of this link between behavior (doing what is right) and emotions in the account of how God dealt with Cain. "The Lord looked with favor on Abel and his offering, but on Cain and his offering he did not look with favor. So Cain was very angry, and his face was downcast. Then the Lord said to Cain, 'Why are you angry? Why is your face downcast? If you do what is right, will you not be accepted? But if you do not do what is right, sin is crouching at your door; it desires to have you, but you must master it'" (Genesis 4:4b-7).

The power to do what is right and the power to resist temptation to sin comes from yielding to God. When a person submits or yields control to Jesus Christ as Lord, he is empowered by the indwelling Holy Spirit to do the right thing, and right behavior pays good dividends in the emotional life.

2. Be Honest About Your Feelings

The second action for managing emotions is a *heart* strategy. It involves honest, intimate communication when you put feelings into words and share them. It is communication from one person's heart to another. Honesty is a key principle in this action. This important practice is your second pathway to changing your emotions. The process of putting your feelings into words and sharing them with another person is a primary God-given means to help you manage your emotions. The ideal is when you believe that the other person will care for you and respond with love and grace. There is something very healing about confessing emotions in words to another person and having them care. God created Adam as a relational being. He said that it was not good for man to be alone and gave him a helper

(Genesis 2:18). God has designed three significant and exclusive relationships for making this kind of emotional connection. Experiencing this type of healthy intimate fellowship and interaction can lift emotional burdens and reduce your discomfort, pain and distress.

The first and most important intimate level of relationship is with God. The second is found in marriage and the third is within a local fellowship of believers in the church. I will develop how to cultivate the second and third levels of relationship latter.

Most fundamental to all your relationships is having a transparent, intimate, and dynamic relationship with God where you share emotions from your heart. God has promised to treat you with honesty, care and grace. He has both designed you for this and desires to enjoy this kind of emotional intimacy with you. It is also a pivotal practice in managing your emotions.

Within this relationship of emotional honesty and intimacy you can, as King David put it, "pour out your heart" to God. He invites each of us to share things with Him that we can share with no one else. Jesus invites all to come to Him and experience intimacy and rest. "Come to me, all you who are weary and burdened, and I will give you rest" (Matthew 11:28-30). David says, "Find rest, O my soul, in God alone;" and instructs believers to follow his example when he said, "Trust in Him at all times, O people; pour out your heart to Him" (Psalm 62:5 & 8).

David models how to do this in the Psalms. Note his honest words in Psalm 142.

> *"I cry aloud with my voice to the LORD;*
> *I make supplication with my voice to the LORD.*
> *I pour out my complaint before Him;*
> *I declare my trouble before Him.*
> *When my spirit was overwhelmed within me,*
> *You knew my path.*
> *In the way where I walk*
> *They have hidden a trap for me.*
> *Look to the right and see;*
> *For there is no one who regards me;*
> *There is no escape for me;*
> *No one cares for my soul.*

I cried out to You, O LORD;
I said, "You are my refuge,
My portion in the land of the living.
Give heed to my cry..." (Psalm 142:1-6a).

Notice David's skillful way of putting his emotions into words. His words are filled with feelings as he expresses his personal struggles to God. Psalm 55 is another wonderful example that you can learn from as you develop this skill. Listen to David's prayer that is filled with emotion as he cries out to the Lord and then ends with a teaching for others in verse 22, and a personal testimony of faith in verse 23.

"Listen to my prayer, O God, do not ignore my plea; hear me and answer me. My thoughts trouble me and I am distraught..."My heart is in anguish within me; the terrors of death assail me. Fear and trembling have beset me; horror has overwhelmed me. I said, '"Oh, that I had the wings of a dove! I would fly away and be at rest – I would flee far away and stay in the desert; I would hurry to my place of shelter, far from the tempest and storm.'""

"Cast your cares on the Lord and he will sustain you; he will never let the righteous fall...But as for me, I trust in you" (Psalm 55:1-2, 4-6, 22-23 NIV).

I am grateful to God for the Psalms because they show me how to practice this important spiritual, relational, and emotional discipline. If you are a slow learner when it comes to putting your feelings into words (as I have been), you can use the words of David in the Psalms to prime the pump and get started. Identify how he moves, sometimes quite rapidly, from heart expressions of distress to faith and then to truth statements of conviction and testimony.

I believe that it was this kind of intimacy with God coupled with David's love for righteousness that prompted the writer in Scripture to say of him, "the Lord has sought out a man after his own heart" (1 Samuel 13:14).

Cultivate your own intimate walk with God. Then be open and prepared to come seeking help for your own sake and then to aid others in the processing of their emotional distress.

3. Telling Yourself The Truth

The Bible has much to say about the importance of your thoughts and beliefs. It gives abundant and clear instruction that your thoughts are important. This work of doing reality testing with your thoughts is strategic and for most people can be a real ongoing battle. You and I are bombarded with lies and deceptive thoughts that must be challenged. God can speak truth into your life through the Bible. He can also use others to speak truth to you as well. I like to call this the work of reality testing. You and I are in constant need of being reminded of what is true and what is not. This inner battle for the truth is both a spiritual and a mental health issue. When your mind dwells on that which is false, it is costly in many ways. Let your mind dwell on what is true (Philippians 4:8).

Jesus said that the devil is "the father of lies" (John 8:44). John spoke of him as the one "who deceived" (Revelation 20:10). Believing his lies has consequences for now and for eternity. He is also called "the accuser" (Revelation 12:10). Satan means "accuser" in Hebrew, and devil means "accuser" in Greek. Satan's goal is to accuse, deceive and destroy (John 10:10; 1 Peter 5:8).

Satan is constantly trying to get individuals to believe false accusations against God, oneself, and others. When his tricks succeed and you believe his lies, he will produce an incredible amount of pain and destruction. Believing any lie plays right into his hand. He is a master in this arena. As any lie is rehearsed over time it grows in power. Repeating thoughts that are untrue is dangerous. Your primary battle is in the mind. Although Satan was defeated on the cross, he remains an active foe.

Dwelling on truth, on the other hand, brings blessing from God. The most obvious way to do this is to meditate on the truth of Scripture (Psalm 19:7-11). Jesus prayed, "Sanctify them by the truth; your Word is truth" (John 17:17). God the Holy Spirit takes the Word of God and applies it to where change is needed. He shapes and molds you like a potter shaping a clay vessel, making you useful to Him by transforming and renewing your mind (Romans 12:2).

Learning to identify a lie and replace it with the truth is one of the key disciplines of life. In my experience working with people, I have found that when I have invited a person to articulate some secret thought they have been thinking, very often they will realize that it is not true and that it does not correspond to reality. They may even begin to laugh as they hear it said for the first time out loud. They begin to realize how ludicrous it sounds when put into words.

Some lies start out small and grow, like stories about fishing. The fish that got away seems to grow larger each time the story is told. In the same way, as a lie is repeatedly told inside your private thoughts, it gets further from the truth and gains more and more power. The lie will continue to exert negative influence and inflict greater damage as it produces negative and twisted feelings. Secret lies that are rehearsed in the mind call for brutal honesty or they will hold you a prisoner to self-defeating thoughts and emotions. Repeating a lie gives the devil the power to keep you defeated.

This work of testing reality in the thought life is essential for spiritual and emotional health.

Thinking, Feeling and Choosing

A good way to think about human personhood is to understand that God created man as a living soul with the capacity to think, feel, and choose. This is why I keep returning to this basic model to frame and inform intervention strategies around the head, the heart, and the hands.

It is good to be reminded that sin distorts these capacities. Many people are stuck in maladaptive habits in one or more of these critical arenas. Christ liberates and He often uses a well-equipped and growing believer to come alongside and minister help.

Chapter 3

The Fragility and Power of Identity

Stress erodes your confidence because it attacks your personal sense of competency. This erosion, if not well managed, can challenge your very identity. The loss of control over events can lead to a host of negative emotions including hopelessness. This dynamic can quickly activate a downward pressure on your sense of well-being, personal worth and self-esteem. For many people it is only a few short steps from losing control of some significant event, to experiencing an avalanche of negative thoughts and feelings which can quickly create a flood of self-berating thoughts that can mire the person into the bog of self-loathing gloom. The problem is that personal self-worth, value and identity are often tied to personal performance and achievement. Stress can push you down the ladder a few rungs or even leave you in a state of despair. It can feel like the ladder has been kicked out from under you.

A Flawed Basis of Self Worth

Bill had always struggled with the haunting questions, "Who am I and what am I worth?" He spent much of his energy trying to prove that he was somebody worth respecting. As a child he had heard many messages that belittled and scolded him to do better if he was going to amount to anything in life. He threw himself into activities like sports and academics, accumulating the best of everything, and trying to get to the top of his profession. As he reached middle age, he began to have serious doubts. Was all the effort worth it? Were his accomplishments getting him closer to answering his most basic life questions? Bill made a fundamental mistake. He believed the lie that identity and worth are found in accomplishment. His thinking had been shaped by a culture that places a high value on self-effort, accomplishment, and success. When Bill would do something in line with his expectations, he would feel good about himself. And when he fell short of his standard, he would feel worthless and his self-esteem would drop. His conclusion was that he did not measure up. (More of Bill's story is found in the "Stories that Illustrate" section.)

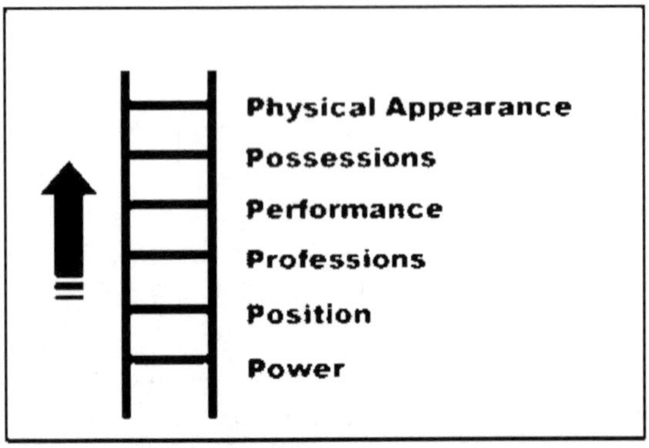

Viewing yourself on an imaginary ladder of self-worth and self-acceptance based upon achievement may provide some temporary relief when things are going well, but this way of thinking is flawed. It is one of the devil's oldest lies. The truth is accomplishment cannot make you okay. It cannot give true identity and worth. No matter how high Bill climbed on his self-constructed ladder there was always a paralyzing fear of falling back down through some misstep. Life on the ladder is precarious.

On good days when Bill thought he was doing well he would look for people around him who, in his eyes, didn't measure up and make fun of them. When he saw himself as nearing the top, in comparison to others, he would become judgmental and difficult to be around. On days that he saw himself as low on the ladder he would throw rocks of criticism, trying to bring others down to his level. People with a ladder mentality often have difficulty in maintaining healthy relationships. Jealousy, envy, pride, lack of humility, and covetousness are all symptoms of ladder thinking. This is an important factor in understanding how stress affects relational peace.

The Greatness of Grace

There is a better way. It is the way of grace. God's grace is based on *what Christ has* done not on what we do. God imputes the righteousness of Christ to us and that demolishes ladder thinking. My identity is safe in Christ. The Apostle Paul declares the truth that by grace and through faith a person is united with Christ and therefore the believer is not under condemnation (Romans 6:5-7; 8:1). The believer's identity is safely hidden in Christ. His work on the cross of making atonement for sin is a finished work, making the believer completely acceptable to God. He has done the work to rescue you from both the penalty and power of sin. Being united with Christ, you share in His accomplishment of keeping the law perfectly. Being in Christ, you stand in His righteousness before God. His righteousness is imputed to you, the believer. In Christ, you share in His resurrected life and will share in His future glory that will soon be revealed. The phrase, "in Christ," was one of the Apostle Paul's favorite ways of expressing this important theological truth. The identity and worth of the believer is secured by our position of being in Christ. God has, by His grace, "seated us with Him (Christ) in the heavenly realms" (Ephesians 2:4-9).

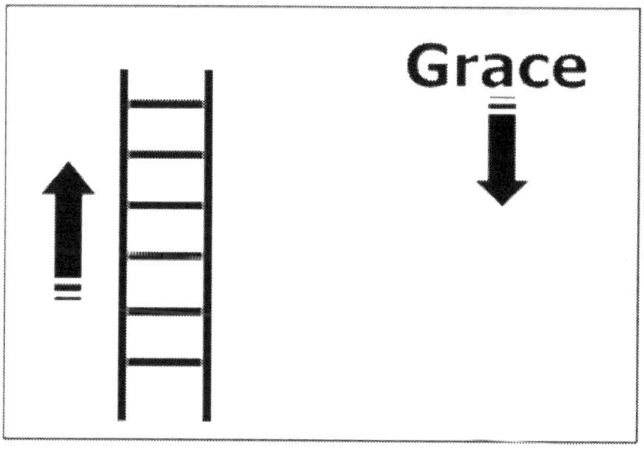

In the Garden of Eden, the devil offered Eve a cheap substitute, a false shortcut to greatness, a plan of self-elevation to become "like God" (Genesis 3:5). Every false religion is some kind of variation on this self-elevation theme. Man universally wants to believe that he is capable to save himself through his own good works. Self-elevation is at the center of our fallen nature. God's plan of salvation calls the individual to give up that flawed idea and cry out in faith for His mercy and the salvation offered to those who believe in Christ. This promise is for all who personally put their only hope in the sufficiency of the finished work of Christ on the cross.

Jesus' harshest words were for the Pharisees, who had taken the Law of Moses and turned it into a performance ladder of self-accomplishment (Matthew 23:1-36). In the Sermon on the Mount, Jesus demonstrated that they were not made righteous in their attempt to keep the Law (Matthew 5:20-48). Six times He repeats the phrase, "You have heard that it was said," followed by a clear reference to some aspect of the Law. Jesus, then said, "but I tell you," six times. Each of the statements that followed made it obvious that no one following a ladder system of righteousness would achieve right standing before a Holy God. I encourage you to study this important passage of Scripture. The Apostle Paul summarized this same truth. "Now we know that whatever the law says, it says to those who are under the law, so that every mouth may be silenced and the whole world held accountable to God. Therefore no one will be declared righteous in his sight by observing the law; rather, through the law we become conscious of sin" (Romans 3:19-20).

James adds, "For whoever keeps the whole law and yet stumbles in just one point is guilty of breaking all of it" (James 2:10).

Every person has inherited, along with the rest of the human race, this deeply embedded rebellion against the need for grace. Mankind stubbornly holds on to the belief that they can climb the ladder of self-justification; that you can become a person of worth and value if they just do enough good, have enough success, or perform well enough on their imaginary ladder. Human pride and the world's value system say that a person is good enough to do it on their own if they just try hard enough. This self-elevation system that excludes God and puts man at the center is called humanism. It shows itself in every culture of the world and surfaces within every individual. It stands at the core of man's rebellion against God.

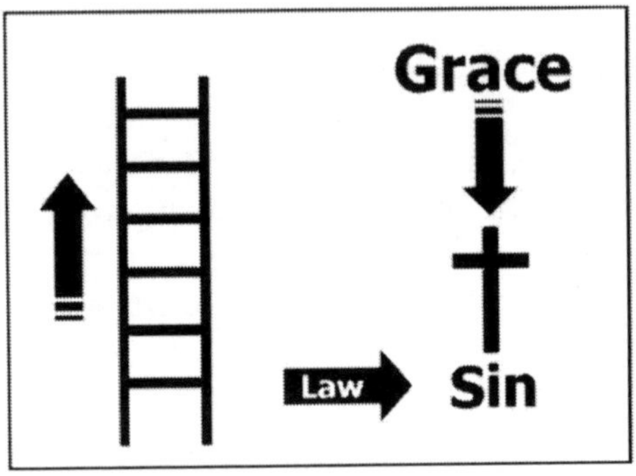

The Law points out that all have sinned and stand in need of God's provision of grace. The gift of God is Jesus Christ's work on the cross to provide salvation to everyone who will believe. My experience is that many people who understand grace for salvation fail to live out grace in other areas of life. They continue to live as if the ladder system is valid for their self-worth and identity. They have become slaves of the ladder mentality and are living defeated lives. Paul warns us to not return to a works-oriented way of life and the burden of slavery it brings (Galatians 5:1).

Four Key Areas of Application for Grace Living

Applying this truth to four basic areas of life is critical. First is the area of physical appearance, athletic ability and mental giftedness. This gets started early in life. Children and young people are especially vulnerable to this way of thinking because of society's constant drumbeat of competition and hero worship. School children can tell you where they stand on these ladder comparisons to the other children in their classroom or on the ball field. The world ranks everyone into categories. Children unsuspectingly fall right into this trap. As a parent you must help your children identify this dangerous and debilitating lie. Teach them to contrast it with the truth of the doctrine of common grace. God has designed and created each individual (including your child) to be unique. His plan is good (Psalm 139:13-16). The truth is that every person has worth and value because they are created in the image of God and are part of His creation. When you are tempted to think self-deprecating or damaging thoughts you can identify the source of those thoughts and replace them with truth statements from Scripture. This is how Jesus responded to the temptation of the devil as recorded in Scripture (Matthew 4:1-10). Speak the truth out loud. This helps you hear the words. An example of this self-talk might sound like this, "I am a special creation of God. God loves me and has created me to be unique. He has a purpose for me to bring Him glory. I have worth and value."

The second area of application is to remember that salvation is not by human works, but rather is given as a gift of God's grace by trusting in Christ's finished work on the cross (Ephesians 2:8-9). Understanding that your salvation is being safely hidden in Christ is most basic to defending and rejecting the devil's use of ladder thinking when he accuses you of not measuring up (usually when you are under stress). When this occurs you can identify the dynamic of what is happening and take action by speaking the truth you know to be true. Repeating this truth in a simple statement is a good way to reinforce it. Say something like, "By faith I am in Christ and therefore, can enjoy this special position of being in God's family, this is His grace gift to me and not based on my works" (Galatians 4:4-7). A realization of this truth can be transforming. Resting by faith in His provision brings great peace. What could be greater than being an heir of God and a fellow heir with Christ (Romans 8:17)? This should cause all human accomplishments to fade in comparison with the wonderful position of exaltation one has in Christ. Your identity is secure. It is not based on your accomplishments but on Christ's and your being united with Him.

The third crucial area where ladder thinking often creeps in is in the application of the doctrine of sanctification. When this doctrine is turned into a ladder, or a works system of self-elevation, people become proud of their spiritual accomplishments and also vulnerable to fear that they might lose their gains by some false step or failure. The Bible says clearly that, "God opposes the proud" (1 Peter 5:5). It is true that sanctification is progressive and calls you to say no to sin and yes to God. It is a grace work of God in our lives to make you Christ-like. God's work is good and He will complete it. He calls the believer to agree and say no to sin and yes to Him each day (Ephesians 2:10, Philippians 1:6, 1 John 3:2-3). The devil stands ready to accuse you if and when you move back to a ladder way of thinking about your sanctification.

The fourth area where many stumble back into a ladder way of thinking is in the area of giftedness and service for Christ. It seems at times churches becomes so enamored with certain gifts or with successful and gifted people that service is turned into a measure of spirituality. Gifts and giftedness can become a basis for pride. It is interesting that the Greek word for gifts is "grace." Servants of Christ need to tell themselves often that God has given these gifts, abilities, and opportunities to serve and not to be used to climb a ladder or as a way to improve their self-esteem. Gifts are to be used to serve others and bring glory to God, not to raise low self-esteem. True service for Christ and bearing spiritual fruit is possible only by God's grace working in and through the individual as you abide in Christ (John 15:4, 8). There is no room for pride.

Action Steps

In response to this section, take some action steps in applying these important truths. Ask God to convict you or help you identify some area of your life where ladder thinking has taken hold. Reject it and begin to cultivate a new way of grace thinking. Practice telling yourself the truth; rejoice in His grace and rest in His acceptance. In Christ you have identity, worth, and validity. You do not deserve it. You may be tempted to doubt it. But you would be a fool not embrace it and enjoy your relationship with Him, the giver of all that is good. Your identity in Christ should be your most precious possession.

Reflect and Discuss:

1) If you could change anything about your physical appearance, would it make you feel better about yourself?

2) Do you ever put yourself down for not being as smart or good-looking as others?

3) Are you envious of the talent, giftedness and success of others?

4) How much material wealth would it take for you to feel important?

5) How much good would you have to do to be accepted into heaven by God?

6) What head, heart and hands action steps can you take to apply this truth to yourself?

Section II

Keys to Stress-Proofing Your Relationships

The previous chapters have mainly dealt with your personal life. The concepts covered in Section I provide the foundation for relational peace and Section II builds upon these important earlier concepts. The personal discipline for ordering your private inner world cannot be off-loaded to anyone else. It is a personal responsibility. Solomon said it like this, "Watch over your heart with all diligence, for from it flow the springs of life" (Proverbs 4:23).

In Section II the focus moves to behaviors that promote and undergird your relationships. I have chosen to use the "walking" metaphor because it is often used in the Bible to refer to a person's manor of life. Today the term "life-style" captures the idea quite well. Why only include six areas? It is true that all of life could be included because all of life touches our relationships. My desire is to highlight what I believe are keys that I have observed in successful people that God has wonderfully blessed in building His church. The Bible also puts emphasis on each of these.

Chapter 4 - Walking Together

Chapter 5 - Walking in the Light

Chapter 6 - Walking in Respect

Chapter 7 - Walking in Love

Chapter 8 - Walking in Forgiveness

Chapter 9 - Walking in Partnership

Chapter 4
Walking Together

The first and most basic principle of relationship is that both parties must agree to **walk together.** We could put the question simply as; "Is there commitment to the relationship?" Amos the prophet, speaking for God, asked the people of Israel the question like this, "Do two walk together unless they have agreed to do so" (Amos 3:3 NIV)?

It is always important to look at the historical context of a passage of Scripture before making application. This is true of Amos 3:3. The prophet Amos was speaking for God. He was calling the people to restore broken fellowship. This is a central message of all the Old Testament prophets as God spoke through them to call His people to restoration of fellowship. I think this text as well as many other passages in the Old Testament Prophets is teaching the "reconciliation principle." God is calling His people back into fellowship. They had sinned and broken fellowship with God.

Relationship and Fellowship

It is helpful to note that there is a difference in the Bible between relationship and fellowship. In the Old Testament God made an unconditional promise to Abraham. This covenant was unilateral and promised to bless Abraham, his offspring and the world through his seed (Genesis 12:1-3; 15:17-18 and 17:1-8). God called him to be the father of a nation that would bring the Messiah and salvation to the world. He also promised a Kingdom ruled from Jerusalem that is yet to come. The nation had a special covenant relationship with God and He will accomplish what He has promised. This, however, did not guarantee personal salvation for every individual in Israel. We are told that Abraham "believed in the Lord; and He reckoned it to him as righteousness" (Genesis 15:6). Personal salvation in both the Old and New Testaments was by grace through personal and individual faith or belief.

In the New Testament this is expanded and clarified. Here we discover that a right relationship with God is through personal faith or belief in Jesus Christ the Savior that God has provided. Those who have entered into that relationship are referred to in different ways but all speak of knowing Christ. They are called saints, believers, followers of Christ, children of God, etc. Paul's favorite phrase (as already mentioned) "in Christ" or "in Him" is found some 130 times (27 in Ephesians alone) when speaking about individuals being "united with Christ" by faith (Romans 6:3-5). Jesus used the term "born again" (or born from above) and "born of the Spirit" when speaking with Nicodemus (John 3:3-8). The Gospel of John was written as an evangelistic tract on how to come into this right relationship with God by personal belief in Jesus. John in his gospel uses the word "believe" about one hundred times. It is the key word in his gospel (good news) presentation. "He who believes in the Son has eternal life…" is just one example (John 3:36). John also speaks about walking in fellowship with God for fruitfulness (John 13-17). This theme is developed as walking in the light of authentic fellowship with God that gives both confidence and assurance of salvation to the believer in the epistle he wrote (1 John). Many today get confused about this distinction and merge the believer's position in Christ (relationship with God through Christ) and walking in the light of fellowship with God. Unfortunately, there are many church people who are walking in confusion and defeat. They have come to believe in Jesus as Savior but are not walking in fellowship with Him, not bearing fruit and enjoying the relational peace that that comes from walking in the light (1 John 1:5-7). Like the church of Corinth, they are experiencing much relational discord and the dysfunction that comes with little spiritual maturity (1 Corinthians 3:1-4). The nation of Israel from the time of Abraham had a special collective covenant relationship with God but most did not enjoy fellowship with God or walk with Him as illustrated by the prophets' ministry of calling them back into obedience and fellowship. While a minority within this collective group were individual people of faith who walked with God (Hebrews 11), most of them showed themselves not to be true spiritual faith-descendants of Abraham (1 Corinthians 10:5).

The question asked by God in Amos 3:3 is rhetorical and designed to make the people take stock in the state of their personal relationship and fellowship with God. They assumed everything was fine but God was revealing that there was a very real problem. Amos makes a shocking announcement. He proclaims that God will bring judgment upon this chosen nation. How could this be? God was declaring that the situation had deteriorated to such an extent that He was going to take drastic action. He continued, "Therefore this is what the Sovereign LORD says: '"An enemy will overrun your land, pull down your strongholds and plunder your fortresses.'" The problem was quite simple – the people of Israel had failed in their obedience to the Mosaic covenant with God which promised blessing for obedience and curses for disobedience.

Unlike the unconditional covenant God made with Abraham, the Mosaic covenant was conditional. They had quickly signed onto it as they thought they could keep it. But in reality it only exposed their hard hearts toward God. They failed its demands and rather than calling on God's mercy and grace most failed to receive personal salvation as Abraham had through belief. They saw no benefit from walking in fellowship with God and showed no desire to walk together in fellowship with Him. Most important the hearts had not been changed through personal faith and belief. They needed a new heart which God promised in the new covenant (Ezekiel 36:22-28; Jeremiah 31:31-33). This biblical background teaches us a great deal about all human relationships.

Walking Together in Marriage

Relationships only work when both parties agree to walk together. On occasion in the past when doing marriage counseling I would find that there was so much individual dysfunction that I would tell the couple that they needed to work alone on some personal issues before we could make progress for successful work on the marriage. Marriage counseling doesn't fix individual issues. The risk is to fall into finger-pointing and self-righteous blaming.

Take time to review and assess the personal dynamics that you bring to your relationships. Use the head–heart–hands method. Ask questions like:

1) What beliefs do you hold that need to change?

2) What is the condition of your heart?

3) Have you been born again? Do you have eternal life?

4) What hurt feelings are you holding that are straining transparency?

5) What passions own your heart (good or evil)?

6) What beliefs and behaviors are negatively influencing or pressing upon your relationships?

Would a review of Section be helpful?

Sometimes it should be said by counselors and pastors that marriage counseling can only be effective when both individuals are willing to work together to solve the issues. It is not uncommon for an individual to come alone to seek help for a marriage problem. The appropriate question must be, "Is your spouse willing to come and work together with you?" This is the first and most basic issue in any relationship – are you willing to walk together?

I am not suggesting that if there is resistance at this point one can or should simply walk away. This does, however, help put the focus on what you can do. You can throw yourself upon the mercy of God. Dependence upon God is always the right place to start. Pray that God will move the other person's heart to be willing to work together with you and walk together toward restoration of fellowship. You can break down your prayers into small steps such as attending one meeting to explore one or two objectives to move the relationship forward. Then agree to take another step together. Walking happens one step at a time. Make sure that you bathe each step in prayer.

Marriage begins with a commitment. More precisely a Christian marriage is a covenant which is made between a man and a woman in the sight of God. It is so important that you ask God, family and friends to serve as witnesses to the vows that you make. Most simply put, it is a promise to walk together in an exclusive relationship for the rest of your natural life. This serves as protection and security for the individuals in the family and the relationship as well. It provides a context where love, peace, and joy can flourish. I will have more to say about the security that comes from practicing healthy boundaries in a later chapter, but a good starting point is considering the insecurity that comes from living under the threat of someone getting mad and walking out. Idle threats about divorce in the heat of an argument should be off limits.

Walking Together in the Church

The local church is another arena where the commitment to walk together is vital. I have served seven churches as pastor and have watched people leave the church over various conflicts, some of which were quite trivial. A contributing factor today seems to be a thin commitment to walk together in a local fellowship. Many think it is easier to just start over and attend another church across town or down the street. The stated reasons for leaving may be a general, "our needs are just not being met," but often there is more to the story. What is lurking under the surface that remains unspoken? It can be hurt feelings from a thoughtless offensive remark, the style of worship service, poor teaching, lack of warmth, or the personality or style of a leader.

As a young pastor I took it too personally each time an individual or family left the church. Sometimes I could identify what had gone wrong but often I was left guessing. The lack of commitment to walk together in fellowship and work through issues was almost always a significant part of the equation.

One of my conclusions is that thriving churches work to form and maintain a healthy partnership between the pastor and the people. When that partnership goes sour there are lots of problems. Not unlike a marriage, church relationships can get ugly, complicated and confusing. I will have more to say in chapter Chapter 9 about the importance of partnerships, but here I want to underscore how fundamentally important commitment is to any relationship. Finding ways to state and restate your personal commitment to walk together through good times and bad is an essential practice that promotes long-term relational peace.

Many passages in the New Testament flesh out this concept in practical instruction and warnings to local churches (Galatians 5:15; Ephesians 4:2-6; Philippians 2:1-4; 4:2-3; 1 Corinthians 3:3-3; James 3:1-18; and 1 John 3:16-18). I would recommend returning to these and other passages that teach the importance of the believing community's commitment to walk together in fellowship.

Maintaining Unity

We could sum up this theme with Paul's words, "Make every effort to keep the unity of the Spirit through the bond of peace" (Ephesians 4:3). A good exercise of application would be to stop and identify any relationships where peace would be promoted by simply speaking a few words of loving affirmation and commitment that would clarify or reaffirm your desire to walk together in peace and harmony.

Chapter 5

Walking in The Light

The second principle to stress-proofing your relationships is to **walk in the light.** The Apostle John clearly links relational fellowship with walking in the light. "If we walk in the light, as he is in the light, we have fellowship with one another" (1 John 1:7). John states his purpose in writing near the end of his letter. "I write these things to you who believe in the name of the Son of God so that you may know that you have eternal life" (1 John 5:13; John 5:24). He is answering a basic question that people have asked for ages, "How can you know that you have a right relationship with God?"

John answers this basic question by pointing the reader to the supporting evidence of love for your brother, not loving the world, but rather walking in love, obedience and righteousness. These are the confirmations that can be seen in the life of the true believer and follower of Christ who is walking in fellowship with God. It is a life characterized by love rather than hate for your brother (1 John 2:9-11; 4:20-21). It is living in fellowship with God and His people. It is seeking God by faith (Hebrews 11:6). It is enjoying the new life that He has given. It is resting in the truth that "...God has given us eternal life, and this life is in His Son. He who has the Son has the life; and he who does not have the Son of God does not have the life" (1 John 5:11-12).

The Light of Faith

Seeking God by faith is central to walking with Him in fellowship. It is being in tune with God's Spirit and those who walk with Him. If you see these dynamics in your life – and they are increasing– it will add to your assurance that God has lavished His grace and love on you as His child and that He is transforming you into Christ-likeness. You can look with confidence to the day when He returns and the transformation process in you will be completed (1 John 3:1-3).

John's logic is straightforward; the evidence that you have been born from above is that your life (and certainly your relationships) will be identifiably different from the run of the mill relationships in the world around you. What is promoted as the normal way to do relationships by social media or Hollywood entertainment will stand in opposition to the real thing. Believers who want to stress-proof their relationships will be committed to walking together in the light.

John is not writing about physical light but uses this same metaphor that Jesus used repeatedly of Himself in His teaching (John 3:19-21; 8:12; 11:10; and 12:35-6). Walking in the light, therefore, refers to living in a manner that is consistent with God's character. The statement "God is light and in Him there is no darkness at all" (1 John 1:5) refers, therefore, to God's nature of righteousness, holiness and purity. From the earliest records in Genesis only a few walked by faith and "called upon the name of the LORD," and, (like Enoch), "walked with God" (Genesis 4:26, 5:22 and 24). This concept has mammoth implications for relationships.

Light and Darkness

The commitment to walk together is too often separated from this basic teaching of Scripture that walking in fellowship with God is a walk of faith. If we believe we can walk together in peace and harmony with others apart from walking with God, we will pay the price of strained and fractured relationships. The presupposition here is that true believers cannot walk together in the light of fellowship with God and with those who are in darkness (2 Corinthians 6:14).

That does not mean that we should be unkind or ill-mannered toward anyone who is still in darkness. We are to extend God's love and light to all with a winsome spirit. The love in our hearts, words, and actions toward those still in darkness must match the gospel of grace that we proclaim. Being in the world but not of the world is not always easy. Here, however, we are speaking about an intimacy or a bond of fellowship that is unique and exclusive for those within this redeemed community.

Jesus taught His disciples that they would be excluded from fellowship with the world. Indeed they should expect to be hated by the world because the world hated Jesus (and still does). There are practical relational implications for those who commit to walk in the light of fellowship with God. You will be hated at a very basic level. This is an uncomfortable fundamental truth that Jesus clearly taught (John 15:18-25). In His prayer in John Chapter 17 Jesus prayed for protection for His own while they are in this world and that they should "be brought into complete unity" with other true believers. Notice the relational language that permeates this text, "…that they may be one as we are one; I in them and you in Me. May they be brought to complete unity to let the world know that You sent Me and have loved them even as You have loved Me" (John 17:22-23).

You may be thinking, "What is the exclusive fellowship that believers in Christ share?" It is a restored or reconciled relationship. That takes us back to the beginning – to creation and the fall of man (Genesis 1-3). "Then God said, 'Let Us make man in Our image'" (1:26-27; also note; 2:7; 17-18; 24). The first thing we note is the use of the plural "Us" and "Our" (26). How is man different from the rest of creation? He was made in the image and likeness of God as a moral, spiritual, and relational being with the capacity (as a personal being in the image of God), to think, feel and choose. This is why I have built my memory hooks around use of the *head, heart and hands*. God is One and exists eternally in three Persons (Father, Son, and Holy Spirit). Within the three Persons of the Godhead – God has existed eternally in holiness and moral perfection, enjoying perfect relationship and fellowship, as a community of love and communication within Himself before the creation of the world. The three Persons of the Godhead each have the capacity to think, feel and choose. In theological talk personhood is described as the capacity to think, feel and choose. God created man in His image and likeness with this capacity, however limited we are as finite human relational beings.

Light vs. Lies

In Genesis Chapter 3 we are introduced to another created spiritual personal being. He is the crafty serpent; a powerful (but limited in power) finite angelic creature. Satan spoke to Eve and twisted God's words into a lie. That is what he always does as the father of lies. His purpose is to cause doubt about the intentions of God and therefore undermine God's character of goodness. He is always busy enticing individuals to sin and trying to destroy fellowship between God and man. He continues today as our adversary tempting individuals to indulge in sinful rebellion against God.

Adam and Eve exercised their free will by eating the forbidden fruit. This moral choice to rebel against God resulted in consequences for all of mankind. The results were profound and long-standing, including spiritual and physical death and relational estrangement. Adam and Eve hid themselves from God as they became aware of their new state of moral guilt and shame. Anyone who works with members of this fallen human race understands the pervasive problem of guilt and shame and how destructive they are to all relationships.

Blame is also an important part of this story – Adam blamed Eve and Eve blamed the serpent. The human race has struggled ever since with blame as a caustic and recurring element in relationships. The most significant result, however, was spiritual and physical death. Spiritual death is separation from God. Physical death is the separation of the soul and the body. Death has remained one of mankind's greatest enemies, only being answered by the victory over death at the resurrection of Jesus Christ, giving the believer hope of a resurrected and glorified body for life beyond the grave (1 Corinthians 15:54-57; John 11:25-26).

The God of Relationship

Darrell W. Johnson in his excellent book *Experiencing the Trinity* provides some great insights. This short little book is a great read and has helped me understand the beauty of what God invites the believer to experience. Johnson puts it this way, "The living God is not a solitary God. The living God is not an isolated God. From all eternity the living God has lived in relationship – indeed, has lived as relationship. At the center of the universe is relationship."

"From all eternity the living God has been a relational family. From all eternity the living God has been infinitely pleased as Father, Son, and Holy Spirit."[1] In Chapter 4, Johnson uses seven words to describe what it is like within the fellowship circle of this family: intimacy, joy, servanthood, purity, power, creativity, and peace. God is not needy or lonely. In His wisdom, and grace He has made provision through Christ to draw us into His circle of fellowship. This is what John is speaking about in 1 John Chapter .

It is worth doing a study of the Scriptures that speak of this unique fellowship taking special note of Jesus' instruction on the topic as recorded by the Apostle John. Remember it was with John that Jesus had a very close relationship. John was described as, "the disciple whom Jesus loved" (John 21:7). Note how much attention John focuses on the wonderful fellowship of love, joy, peace, and light (I John 1:3- 2:2; 2:9-10; John 14:20-21, 23; 26-27; 15:5; 8; 11; 17; and 13:34). Also, note how other Scriptures return to these themes to instruct believers about living within this circle of fellowship (1 Timothy 6:16; 1 Thessalonians 5:5; 4:17-5:21; Isaiah 2:5; Romans 12:18; 14:19; 15:13; Ephesians 2:14-17; 4:3; Philippians 1:2; 4:1-2; and Colossians 1:12-14).

[1]*Darrell W. Johnson, Experiencing the Trinity (Vancouver, BC: Regent College Publishing, 2002), selected quotes from pp. 61, 63, 73.*

I think the application is clear – a mutual commitment to walk in the light is foundational to growing any godly relationship. Walking in the light is where love, joy and peace thrive. Say to your spouse, family member, or a fellow believer gathered in the local church congregation, or to a fellow member of your mission team, "I want to live in this zone of fellowship – meet me there and let's walk together in the light – in fellowship with God and each other." Living in the light of God's presence is where relational peace blossoms. It is transformational to relationships. Remember that walking in light drives away the darkness that destroys fellowship.

Chapter 6
Walking in Respect

The third basic principle for stress-proofing your relationships is to **walk in respect.** Managing emotional intimacy is not an easy task. It is this quality that we most hunger for in a relationship, yet it is often the most mysterious, most complicated, and most elusive to master. We long to know and be known – to be accepted and loved. We desire to have someone with whom we can disclose our soul and have the assurance that they will respond with respect, acceptance, genuine interest, and care. We long for emotional bonding.

God has created us with this hunger for connection. As living souls created in the image of God, only He can satisfy this most basic and deepest thirst for relationship. Expecting a spouse (or any human relationship) to completely fulfill this hunger is asking more than any human individual can deliver. Doing so can put great stress on a marriage.

Finding Satisfaction in God First

One of the keys to a healthy marriage is finding one's primary joy, satisfaction, and emotional intimacy in Christ. God intends marriage to provide its own special kind of joy, satisfaction, and emotional intimacy, but it was never meant to be a substitute or replacement for intimate fellowship with God.

Many addictions are driven by attempts to fill the God-shaped vacuum in a person's heart. Material possessions, food, sex, money, drugs, and alcohol are often used in an attempt to fill this void. Pursuing any of these can lead to serious addiction. Substitute pleasures that the world offers are temporary at best, but can become lethal in the end. Science has made great strides in identifying and mapping the pleasure centers of the brain, helping us to understand which chemicals and behaviors trigger them. This can be helpful but is not an ultimate answer. Anything that lures us away from finding our satisfaction in Christ results in emptiness and often leads to bondage. The apostle Paul equates coveting with idolatry (Colossians 3:5). John Piper puts it this way, "Covetousness is desiring something so much that you lose your contentment in God." Christ alone can satisfy and He must be the primary focus of one's

Jesus said, "I am the bread of life. He who comes to Me will never go hungry. And he who believes in Me will never be thirsty" (John 6:35). Only Jesus can satisfy the soul at this deeper level of relationship. As wonderful as marriage is (and it is a great gift from God) it cannot satisfy this primary level of soul hunger. The story of the Samaritan woman at the well is an excellent example of this principle (John Chapter 4).

I believe one of the fundamental problems today is that many people are looking to marriage to satisfy this relational hunger and quench the thirst that only Jesus can satisfy. Anyone who expects a spouse to meet this soul hunger that only God can fulfill will end up disappointed and frustrated.

I remember working with a man who was having an adulterous sexual relationship. We were sitting in a coffee shop when he said to me, "See that door? As every woman enters, I look to see if she is the perfect woman who might satisfy all my needs."

This man's problem was that he was indulging in a fantasy. He chose to believe a common lie. He knew it was wrong, but it had become a habit for him. It was a longstanding mental temptation that he entertained and had rehearsed for years. He cultivated this fantasy by coveting what was not his, and by believing that having it would bring joy, satisfaction, and contentment. By acting upon this lie it only brought grief, pain, and suffering to two families. Most adulterous affairs start with someone believing some variation of this lie.

Intimacy and satisfaction with Jesus bring peace, joy, and contentment that prepare a person for marriage, and safeguard against a potential affair. Intimacy with Christ and desiring to please Him helps a person set good moral boundaries. It also better equips the person to manage intimacy with others. It helps a couple stay in the healthy range of interdependency and protects from the dangerous and unhealthy extremes of relational isolation or enmeshment.

Isolation and Enmeshment

The figure below represents a continuum of emotional closeness. The two extreme ends are both unhealthy. In the middle is a range of interdependency and cooperation. It is where healthy human bonding takes place.

Isolation is when a person retreats from emotional intimacy into distance and coldness, cutting off meaningful communication. People in isolation give the "silent treatment" and become uncooperative, withholding their love and affection. Many marriages are stuck in this cold wasteland, barren of the emotional intimacy and warmth that God desires for married couples to enjoy.

Enmeshment, on the other hand, is a sticky emotional entanglement where the lines between two individuals begin to blur. It is often marked by emotional dependency and neediness. Dependency is when a person expects someone else to do for them that which they should do for themselves. Personal responsibility is offloaded to another. When an individual becomes so needy that they cannot do anything without the emotional support of another, it should raise the caution flag of enmeshment.

Codependency is defined as assuming another person's responsibility and doing for them what they should do themselves. Paul wrote, "…each one should carry his own load" (Galatians 6:5). Those of us who are called to help others occasionally cross the line into unhealthy helping. Someone once said, "Whenever you do something for someone that he should do for himself, you make him an emotional cripple." That may sound harsh and not politically correct by today's standards but there is a measure of truth in the statement that helps identify the danger of co-dependency. You can do too much for people and, in the process, impede their growth into maturity.

A common symptom of both dependency and codependency is controlling or manipulative behavior. It is often in this climate of unhealthy emotional enmeshment where illicit sexual affairs develop.

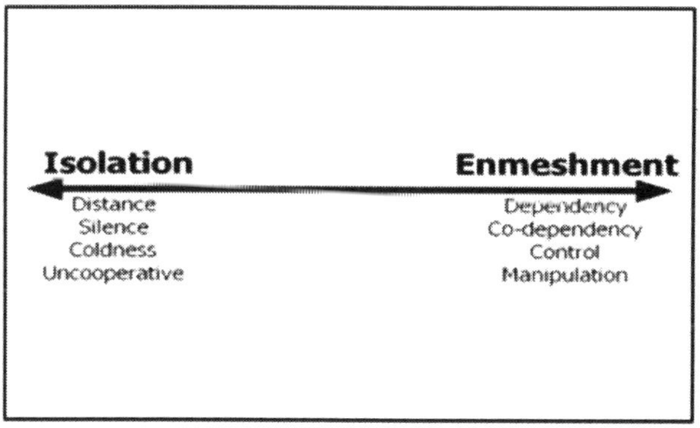

In a marriage, when one partner pulls strongly in one direction and the other pulls in the opposite direction, there is a battle over the practical idea of what is ideal for intimacy. If one wants more space (out of past hurt or fear of being smothered or controlled) and retreats toward the isolation side, the other person may feel like they are being rejected and pull even harder in the opposite direction. The risk is to settle into an unpleasant "tug of war" over emotional closeness and distance. This battle can persist in a marriage for years. Remember that relationships are fluid and there is a natural movement back and forth within the healthy middle range of interdependency. Stress usually pushes people toward the extreme ends of this continuum.

I have found that many couples come to marriage with different expectations about emotional intimacy. They may also come with different communication skills for developing intimacy, diverse ideas about how love should be expressed, and different hopes about bonding. Churches should be supplying skilled helpers to come alongside young couples to help them avoid hitting the rocks in this area. Parents must be having honest conversations with their adolescent children as they become interested in forming emotionally intimate relationships as the world will be sending messages that it is all about sexual intimacy. In Chapter 7 I will discuss how to help people develop better communication skills for emotional bonding. Equally important is gaining a good practical understanding for managing boundaries.

Boundaries

Setting healthy emotional boundaries can help a couple avoid the unhealthy extremes of enmeshment and isolation. Good boundaries help manage the lines of personal responsibility before God who has assigned the marriage partners their respective roles (Ephesians 5:22-31).

Remember that God has chosen to use the husband-wife relationship as an example of Christ's relationship to the Church. Marriage is indeed a sacred trust from the Lord and the Christian couple is called to be good stewards of this wonderful gift. Each individual will have to answer for how he or she has treated the spouse God has provided. The Bible is clear about how your obedience to God will show itself as you love, cherish and respect your spouse (Ephesians 5:22-33). A climate of love and respect characterize every godly marriage.

"Do not let any unwholesome talk come out of your mouths, but only what is helpful for building others up according to their needs, that it may benefit those who listen. And do not grieve the Holy Spirit of God, with whom you were sealed for the day of redemption. Get rid of all bitterness, rage and anger, brawling and slander, along with every form of malice. Be kind and compassionate to one another, forgiving each other, just as in Christ God forgave you" (Ephesians 4:29-32). Walking in respect provides emotional and moral security.

Paul used two different Greek words that are instructive when he wrote, "Each one should carry his own *load*" (Galatians 6:5), also that we are to "Carry each other's *burdens*" (Galatians 6:2). Understanding the difference between these two words is important. In verse 5 the word pictures the idea of a personal knapsack, or individual load, that a person is assigned to carry. We should respect the individual responsibility and not take it from that person no matter how much they complain or fuss. It is their personal responsibility before God. In verse 2 the word used for *burden* is that of a great boulder that could crush the person. In this case we are to put a shoulder under the burden and share the load. Understanding and respecting the difference is extremely important in managing emotional intimacy.

Setting boundaries is about taking personal responsibility. It is not building a wall of separation to hide behind and never help the other. God has called each person in the marriage relationship to lovingly care for and support the other. It is interesting that the Apostle moves from his instruction about submitting to the Holy Spirit and being filled with the Spirit to the theme of worship, and then to the theme of marriage. He begins by giving the insightful command to, "submit to one another out of reverence for Christ" (Ephesians 5:18-21). The Holy Spirit's empowerment is needed to do this well.

The goal is to provide emotional support, love and respect without taking away the spouse's responsibility for healthy management of their own personal emotions. Each individual in marriage needs to learn to find their primary emotional support and intimacy in Christ. Then the individuals can begin to learn how to lovingly serve one another. Remember your spouse may need extra grace and support when they are under the weight of a "stress boulder." The wisdom and daily guidance of the Holy Spirit is indispensable to walk together in loving respect, security and relational peace.

Chapter 7
Walking in Love

The fourth principle to stress-proof your relationships is to **walk in love.** It is connected to respect but I would like to develop this in a separately due to the primary importance of love. I will explore two main thoughts. The first concept is that love involves emotional bonding as we communicate by speaking and listening. In Chapter 6 on respect and boundaries I developed the concept of how bonding can go wrong. Now I will present a quick look at a model for understanding bonding from a healthy perspective. Walking in love starts with respect, but is developed through communication. I will use the heart and head memory hook to aid and clarify.

1. Bonding

Head level communication as seen in the figure below is sharing words and ideas with another person at the thinking level. It involves sharing opinions, concepts, and your thoughts about what you perceive as reality. There is give and take with the other person as they agree or disagree. When they agree you will feel closer and a sense of bonding takes place. It can be said that you fellowship around the ideas you have in common.

Heart level communication is at the feeling level and involves the sharing and caring of feelings. This usually involves a deeper level of bonding. Head level communication involves give and take and requires respect for the other's thoughts and ideas. Heart level connection requires more. It demands respect but must also include caring and empathy.

I have found it helpful to use this visual model of communication to help me understand and practice loving communication for growing intimacy and honesty with another person.

Communication is improved by putting thoughts and feelings into words. The sharing of these words will usually dry up if there is no response from the other person. It takes two persons willing to engage in sharing and responding appropriately for bonding to grow and for the two people to become more emotionally intimate. It is important to recognize that sometimes there is a nuanced difference between the two levels. I have worked with many men who need some coaching at this point. Three good markers for correctly catching the message before you respond are tone of voice, body language, and choice of words. Learning to listen, respect, and respond at the appropriate level is a key to cultivating healthy emotional bonding.

It can be a sign of relational deterioration when one person begins to care more about winning an argument or being "right" than understanding the other person and caring for them. Often our intensity to communicate our ideas comes across like a lecture or an accusation to others. Now it is a short step to crossing the line into bullying others to think and feel like we do. Intensity, volume or overstating our message can create defensiveness in the other person. If we are insecure and have a high need for others to agree with us we may over-sell our idea and simply cause an argument and our stress may push back on our fragile self-esteem. Remember the Stress Cycle can push in both directions.

Missed Connections

This second figure illustrates a common misstep in communication. When one person is on the thinking level and the other person is on the feeling level, connection is not made, and both can leave feeling

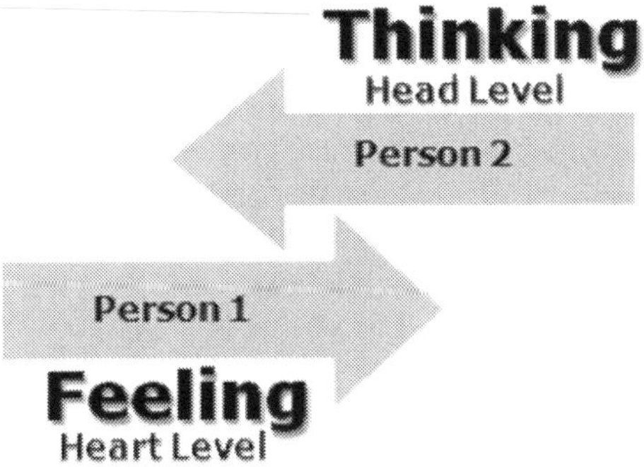

Let me illustrate. Let's say my wife, Bev, returns from a shopping trip and shares with me that she saw, "the most wonderful dress." She may go on to tell me about its lovely color, the texture of the material, how perfect the style was, and even that the size was right for her. After a few minutes, I ask her the price of the dress and instantly jump right to the judgment (thinking level) and say, "Bev, you should know that we cannot afford to buy this dress." Needless to say we are not communicating on the same level. She is at the heart level, sharing her feelings, and I'm at the head level, telling her what I think is the salient truth. I have missed the opportunity to make an emotional connection and bond with her at that moment.

I might respond with an action plan, "What steps do you want me to take to get this done?" "Where can I buy the dress?" At that point she will probably respond by saying, "Lee, I don't want you to buy the dress. I just want you to be happy with me that I found it. I know we can't afford to buy it." She wants me to share her happiness, to enter into her experience of joy, and rejoice with her. Window shopping gives her joy. She wants to connect with me at the emotional level with something she is feeling.

Lecturing others with our opinion of truth may cause us to miss the opportunity to connect with them at the feeling level. Everyone wants to know that someone cares about their feelings. This is one of the reasons why we tell stories; we want someone else to experience things with us. We all want to know that someone cares enough for us to take the time to enter into our feeling world and share our experiences. When I discover some truth in my study, I want someone to listen and rejoice with me in the joy of my discovery.

After we have connected with someone at the feeling level, we can move to the thinking level and deal with truth. Dialogue helps us to sort out what is fact and what is fiction at the head level. This is the hard cooperative work of reality testing. If you move to the thinking level too soon, simply move back to the feeling level to establish additional rapport by expressing empathy.

At the end of a large conference of evangelical leaders in India, Dr. Richard Howell who was at that time the General Secretary of the Evangelical Fellowship of India said to me, "The most important thing that you said to us was to start at the heart and move to the head in working with people."

Speaking the Truth in Love

We need people in our world that will be honest with us. Leaders get into trouble when they don't have people who can speak truth to them. It is dangerous to live in isolation without input from others. You need people who will listen and respond to your ideas, giving feedback when you need a nudge back to reality. One of my favorite verses from the Bible reads, "As iron sharpens iron, so one man sharpens another" (Proverbs 27:17). Don't think this important service is restricted only to those bold abrasive personalities who are always spouting off about their opinion on everything. Managing emotional intimacy requires that you walk in openness and truth. "The LORD God said, 'It is not good for the man to be alone; I will make him a helper suitable for him'" (Genesis 2:18). It is difficult to grow toward spiritual and emotional maturity in isolation. Communication plays an important role in a healthy growing relationship. Healthy communication is at the heart of a healthy relationship.

2. Service

The second concept for walking in love is service. How do we practice this in daily life? What does walking in love look like? Many practical acts of service come to mind but I want to remind you of Jesus' instruction to His disciples in the upper room. He began with what has become a most familiar object lesson – the lowly task of foot washing. The text says, "…having loved His own who were in the world, He loved them to the end" (John 13:1) and then his instruction in verse 14, "If I then, the LORD and Teacher, washed your feet, you also ought to wash one another's feet." This is followed in verse 34 with one of the most quoted directives in the Bible, "A new commandment I give to you, that you love one another, even as I have loved you, that you also love one another."

First, notice that Jesus repeats Himself in verse fourteen. Then again two more times He restates His command (John 15:12 and 15:17). Second, observe that Jesus makes this a "new commandment" which is different from the statement in the law (Leviticus 19:18 and 34). The previous standard was, "you shall love your neighbor as yourself," but now Jesus raises the bar to, "as I have loved you." This is a major change that is often overlooked. Third, watch how often the disciples return to this theme in the rest of the New Testament (Romans 12:10; 13:8; Galatians 5:13; Ephesians 4:2; 1 Thessalonians 3:12; 4:9; 5:13; 2 Thessalonians 1:3; I Peter 4:8; I John 3:11; 23; 4:7; 11-12; and II John 1:5). They got the message and passed it on to the Church.

Debriefing

A practical way to provide loving service is to another person is to practice debriefing. It can help with communication and emotional bonding. The dictionary definition of debriefing, is "to interrogate someone on their return from a mission in order to assess the conduct or results of the mission." You can see the military use in that definition. But the term has come to be used more widely and includes helping a person process their experience following an event. It is this usage that I would like to recommend to you.

In the mid-1980s I began to debrief global servants (missionaries) returning to their home country. Some of them had experienced traumatic events, others had an accumulation of more commonplace stories, but they all longed for someone to listen. Loving service to them meant showing interest in their world by listening. I settled on three questions to ask to get the process started.

1) "What happened?" Or put another way, "Tell me your story."

2) "What did it feel like?"

3) "What conclusions did you draw about your experience?"

Using these three questions, I was inviting the individual to share their events, feelings, and thoughts. I call this the Debriefing Triangle (located in the top right corner of the Stress Cycle as pictured in the following illustration). You can do a lot of listening using only these three questions. Don't hurry the process or ask all the questions at once. Give the person time to reflect and collect their thoughts. Provide time for feelings and memories to resurface. Don't be afraid of periods of reflective silence.

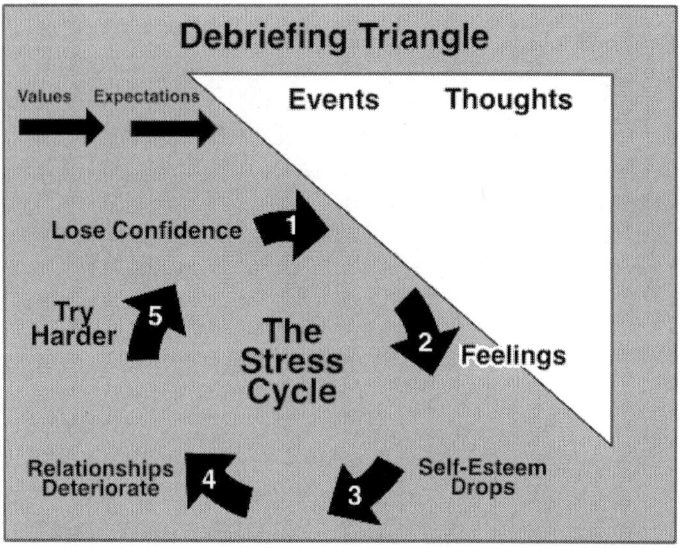

You can also expand your questions by adding variations to the basic three questions. or to other areas of the stress cycle. Some examples might include:

1) Where did this happen?

2) Who else was involved?

3) What did you expect to happen?

4) Why was this important to you?

5) How did it affect your self-concept?

6) How did it affect your relationships?

7) What did it feel like when it took place (then) and what does it feel like now that some time has passed? Have feelings changed?

8) Are there any actions that should be taken?

Debriefing in the Family

In the 1970s and 1980s our daughters were in school. Most days when they returned home, either Bev or I would have a debriefing conversation with them. We tried to use variations of these questions to keep the conversations fresh and relevant. Some examples for kids:

1) "What did your teacher cover in math class today?

2) "How is that history paper progressing?

3) "What do your friends think about that?

4) "How did it feel when she said that to you?"

Doing the work of ongoing debriefing each day will tax your ability to be creative, but it is worth the effort. It will help you bond with your child and help them learn important communication skills for life.

I believe that we need to encourage parents do this with their children. It helps keep communication open between the parent and child. They learn about communication and bonding by watching you model it for them. They learn to tell their stories in words and how to share and process the accompanying thoughts and feelings. For the child, the home should be a safe place to learn how to navigate and share their world. Home is the place kids should learn about good mental health as they process the stuff that happens. This is best done with a caring parent.

Parents need to be careful not to shame the child for processing the event like a child, but should begin to plant seeds of what healthy and mature thinking and feeling are like. As Paul says, "When I was a child, I talked like a child, I thought like a child, I reasoned like a child" (1 Corinthians 13:11). Children process events like children. But over time they begin to learn through interaction with a parent not only how to relate to another person but how to process their world.

Husbands and wives need to learn to debrief each another. Bev and I have learned the importance of taking time to debrief after we have been apart. Having traveled a great deal in ministry, we have found that this helps us in the transitional period of readjustment after returning home. It is not one-sided. We both need to take the time to ask each other the debriefing questions, and then listen attentively as the other person shares.

Debriefing Trauma

Debriefing is extremely important when a person experiences a traumatic event such as an accident, illness, war, persecution, hostage taking, mugging, rape, terrorism attack, earthquake, fire, typhoon, tsunami, etc. The more traumatic the event, the more essential debriefing becomes. Churches should be equipping their people with these skills so that if a widespread disaster occurs there will be Christians ready to step into the gap and serve. Many opportunities can open for the gospel when a local church is equipped and ready to act in times of disaster and serve others in this strategic way.

During a crisis, especially if a person is in shock, attend to immediate physical needs and provide a ministry of presence (stay with a person), when necessary, tell them what to do, and lead them to safety. This is not the time to debrief. This will come later when it is time to reflect back on the event as the person is trying to process it. Debriefing, like all caring ministry, must be done for the glory of God and following His lead. Our objective is to keep God at the center of life and to walk in love and service.

Chapter 8
Walking in Forgiveness

The fifth principle to stress-proof your relationships is to **walk in forgiveness.** Walking in forgiveness brings freedom. It preserves openness and freshness in relationships. Harboring resentment puts a stifling cloud over how you communicate and treat each other. Relationships must be tended within the garden of grace. If a ladder mentality is brought to the relationship, there will automatically be ladder dynamics and conflicts in the relationship. The fruit of criticism, competition, pride, and jealousy will be evident. Ladder thinking coupled with communication that is not based in grace will lead to relational messes. Grace living produces relational peace. Walking in relational forgiveness is an important part of walking in the light and is done best when you incorporate Christ into the relationship.

The Apostle Paul summed it up well, "Be kind to one another, tender-hearted, forgiving each other, just as God in Christ also has forgiven you" (Ephesians 4:32). Solomon wrote, "Two are better than one," and "a cord of three strands is not quickly broken" (Ecclesiastes 4:9 & 12).

The Foundation of Commitment

The foundation upon which relationships are built is commitment, beginning with commitment to God, His grace, and His Word. The foundation of a godly home starts with a commitment to honor God together in everything and by the grace that He supplies. There should be a commitment to study God's Word and apply the truth found there to each and every relationship. Realize that the world's values will often clash with the values of how citizens of heaven should live and treat others (Philippians 2:14, 3:20).

A foundational principle is that each member of the family has dignity before God. A wife is not owned by her husband to meet his every need, but deserves respect as she belongs to God and is a gift of grace to her husband to be a partner in glorifying God together (Proverbs 18:22; 1 Peter 3:7). A husband is not just a bread winner to provide for the family, he too is a gift from God to his wife and is to be highly respected, not held in contempt or belittled as he leads, protects and loves his wife and family even when he does so imperfectly (Ephesians 5:33).

Often what is missing in marriage is a *conscious awareness of Christ's presence*. This is a powerful idea. Bringing Christ into all the activities of a marital relationship can transform how couples live together. When a man is aware of the presence of Christ, he will treat his wife differently than if he thinks no one is looking. Christ is the unseen guest at every meal; He hears every conversation, sees the heart and knows the hidden motives. The home that practices the presence of Christ will begin to reflect godly character and qualities in its relationships.

A commitment to God should, therefore, precede the commitment to one another. God's Word calls a couple to make a till-death-do-us-part covenant (Malachi 2:14). This is a covenant relationship of love, honor, faithfulness and respect that seeks to put the spouse's needs ahead of your own needs (Ephesians 5:21-33). You should keep your focus on God to meet your needs rather than looking to your spouse.

God works through people, but He is the source of every good gift (James 1:17). Looking to Him to supply your needs rather than becoming dependent upon or demanding of your spouse, is a key to godly living. If we shift our eyes away from Jesus and onto each other we will become disappointed and begin to blame and shame one another.

Stress will test the fidelity of this covenant. It takes the grace of God to live it out in long-term reality. This is one of the most God-honoring things we can do on this earth because it reflects Christ's relationship with His bride, the Church (Ephesians 5:22-33).

Resolving Conflict

Conflict resolution is truly an indispensable discipline in preserving a relationship. Conflicts will happen. There will be times you have ideas, judgments, and opinions that differ. It would be nice if everyone agreed with you on everything. That will never happen in this life. To have complete agreement on everything would make us like clones. Again, respect for the uniqueness of your spouse is important. You need to have a plan for dealing with conflict and a firm commitment to use it. Remember the biblical instructions to "be of the same mind toward one another; do not be haughty in mind," and, "if possible, so far as it depends on you, be at peace with all people" (Romans 12:16 and 18). When you read the Bible you see plenty of conflict that you can learn from. There are many good and bad examples. The issue is how to manage them to the glory of God (Acts 6:1-6; 15:37-40). I have found the following model especially useful.

I have used the thinking level/feeling level model (or head level/heart level) as a basic plan to guide in walking through a series of steps toward conflict resolution. It begins with distinguishing between the thinking and feeling levels of conflict. This is important as many times both levels need attention. Prayerfully consider applying the following strategies.

Thinking-Level Strategies

1. Use good communication skills to clarify what each person is really saying. Don't assume you know what the other is thinking. Take the time to listen to each other (James 1:19). Be kind and courteous. Gently share your thoughts and opinions. Keep the lines of communication open. Ask questions to draw out the other person's thoughts. Try to stick to one topic at a time.

2. Don't attribute motives to the other person. Let the person speak and disclose the reasoning behind their actions .

3. Sometimes you can negotiate a solution. Occasionally it is best to compromise and meet in the middle. At times you can collaborate to find a way to work together on the issue. Other times accommodation is the best solution.

4. There will be times, however, that you must realize that you do not have to agree on everything. You can **agree to disagree** and stay in fellowship. "If possible, so far as it depends on you, live peaceably with all" (Romans 12:18). To do this, you can reaffirm your commitment to the other person and your commitment to maintain your relationship with them. You can express this desire by saying, "I respect you, and I want to retain a good relationship with you. I don't want this to come between us. I respect your opinion. Let's agree to disagree on this."

Thinking-level conflicts are easier to resolve than feeling-level conflicts. Things get sticky when they move from the head to the heart. When people become hurt and angry conflict resolution becomes more complicated. It is even more crucial to work a plan. I have found it important to move through these next strategies *sequentially*. Two people can do these steps alone, but sometimes it takes the assistance of a third person to help keep the process on track and walk the two individuals through this process.

Feeling-Level Strategy

1. Start by identifying the emotions of hurt and pain in both persons. J. Grant Howard in his book *The Trauma of Transparency* writes about how people build walls that they hide behind. These walls are an accumulation of hurts that are used as bricks. Occasionally, Howard says, we will reach down, take a brick and hurl it at the other person, using our hurt as a weapon against the other person. We then feel guilty and defensive. The Holy Spirit may be reminding us that we are not practicing what Paul instructed Christians to do (Ephesians 4:32, 1 Thessalonians 5:15).

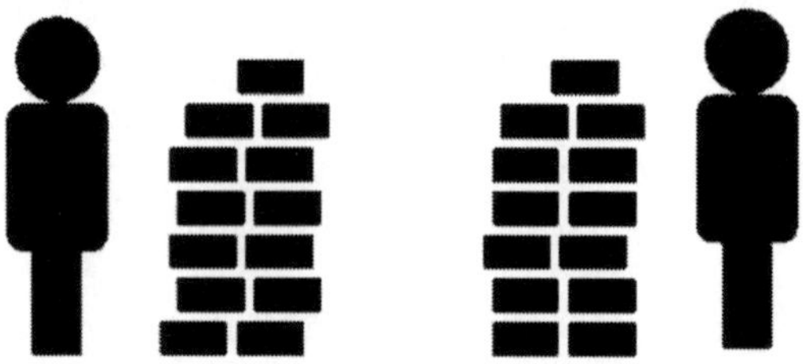

I remember working with two physicians who were at odds with each other and had a reputation for not getting along. Everyone in the hospital knew about their ongoing conflict. We sat down together and walked through these steps. At the point of identifying the feelings of each, one said to the other, "I never knew you felt this way." The other doctor replied, "And I never knew you felt that way."

Honestly sharing how each person feels and taking time to really listen to the other person can be a big step toward healing a fractured relationship. This needs to be done in a safe place where no one gets dumped on by a load of pent-up emotions. No dumping allowed! If a number of hurts have been stored up it is better to go slowly, one at a time, than to dump the whole truckload at once. This is where a wise mediator can be extremely helpful.

2. Express care and concern for the other person's hurt. You can do this without agreeing with the thoughts that generated the feeling.

Honestly say, "I'm sorry that you have been hurt, I want you to know that I care about your feelings." Reach out beyond your personal hurt and focusing on the other person rather than waiting for them to act first. Somebody has to start. It is godly to take the initiative in reconciliation. There is a risk, however, of stopping at this point and not moving on through the next important steps.

3. Take responsibility and ownership for your part in causing the other person's hurt. Jesus said that we are to put a high value on reconciliation (Matthew 5:23-24, 7:3). A practical step in doing this is to identify your role. Most people, being somewhat defensive, have a hard time believing they have caused any part of the pain. It is at this point that one can best serve the other person by humbling oneself and, as it were, washing their feet by asking for forgiveness. This servant role can help prompt the other person to release what they have been holding. Simple words should be used, "Will you forgive me for (state the offense)?"

4. Forgive. Even when the other person does not ask to be forgiven, as Christians we must forgive. It is important to remember that granting forgiveness is an act of the will whereby a person releases what has been held against another's account. Forgiveness in the New Testament is an economic term that means erasing a debt that is owed. Forgiveness is costly. No more debt. No more making them pay.

Use simple words, "I forgive you for (name the offense). I don't want this to be a barrier in our relationship any longer." This is done by faith and in obedience to the command of Scripture (Matthew 18:21-35). The key to forgiveness is coming to understand how much you have been forgiven by God's extension of grace to you. Grasping the magnitude of His grace to cover your sin compels you to extend grace to others. Forgiveness is a mark of understanding grace.

I think it is a good idea to ask God to witness the act of forgiveness. Later if you begin to have doubts about the validity of the transaction, doubting that it was done right or even done at all, you can recall that God indeed was present as a witness to what was said and done.

An example might be to pray, "Heavenly Father, thank You for Your presence with us as we conduct this important business of forgiveness. I want to be clean before You and my brother. Please Lord, be a witness to what we say to each other now as we, in obedience to Your Word, release what we have held against each other. Thank You for Your forgiving grace that teaches us to forgive. For Jesus' sake, Amen."

5. Use the hands, heart, and head approach to managing emotions. Sometimes you will have leftover feelings that hang around for a while. You need to take steps to address these feelings. First, do what is right. Act in a loving way toward the person. Don't avoid them or gossip about them, but rather pray for them and look for ways to do acts of kindness toward them. Second, share leftover feelings honestly with God. He understands your human frailty and weaknesses. Third, tell yourself the truth. Challenge the temptation to go back and rehearse the original offense. Remember that this matter has been dealt with. Forgiveness has been granted and received. Walk in the freedom of that forgiveness.

Chapter 9
Walking in Partnership

The sixth principle to stress-proof your relationships is to **walk in partnership.** "Two are better than one because they have a good return for their labor" (Ecclesiastes 4:9). This biblical passage is frequently used in wedding ceremonies as it goes on to say, "a cord of three strands is not quickly torn apart" (verse 12). It speaks poetically of the partnership principle that produces a multiplier effect. In most areas of life it is true that we can be more productive by working together than we can when working in isolation.

Important Partnerships

Partnership is one of the keys to a good marriage. It is simply working together in cooperation toward a common goal or purpose. The individual roles may differ but the sense of partnership is real. This truth can be seen in a wide range of tasks from simple household chores, to running a family business or rearing children. Many examples could be cited from different cultures from around the world, ranging from caring for animals, tilling crops, to tending a corner store in the marketplace. Church history is also filled with stories of beautiful partnerships between husbands and wives in missionary work as well as local church ministry.

Another important area of partnership is that of the ministry relationship in a local church between a pastor and the people. Establishing and maintaining this partnership is a key to a healthy church. If this erodes there is usually an increase in misunderstandings, breaches of trust, interpersonal tensions and conflict. Soon people start looking for the exit and leave. This, of course, can be very damaging to the testimony of the church and the work of Christ in a community (John 13:35) as well as the damage that is done to individuals and families. The same kind of damage occurs in the missionary context when team partnerships break down. I spent a number of years doing team building and counseling with missionaries and mission groups. Some of the insight in this book grew out of applying these principles within the context of missionary work.

Assessing the health of any partnership is multifaceted. The pastor/congregation relationship has added dimensions and complexity due to respect for biblical mandates regarding spiritual authority not to mention the legal, fiscal, and moral responsibility as required by the principles of good governance. An attorney helped me understand the concept of a limited partnership. It simply means that each partner's contribution will be unique (not equal). This is why it is always important to do a lot of identifying and clarifying of the individuals' roles for each participant. This is how good partnerships are established and maintained. Taking time for good communication to review, evaluate, clarify and adjust expectations and limitations for each person's contribution is time well spent.

This is also indispensable in teamwork and is never completely finished, as team dynamics and individuals change. We should remember that dysfunctional churches existed in the New Testament. Corinth and the seven Churches of Revelation (Chapters 2 and 3) are clear examples.

This subject of building stress-proof relationships is timely due to the divisions that stress is currently bringing to all relationships. Rather than trying to flesh out all possible applications for business partnerships, families, church groups or mission teams, I would suggest that you ask God to guide you as you discuss what next steps your group needs to take. You might begin with a brief introduction of the subjects from this book and explore together what specific points of application would please the Lord of the harvest. Even something as simple as asking the questions:

1) How are the increased levels of stress affecting the way we are doing God's work?

2) Are we collectively modeling biblical relational peace?

Section III

Doing Life for the Long-Haul and Finishing Well

Five Activities that Make a Difference

A new term is being used for promoting life-long health. It is *health span*. The idea is to stay healthy and active in mind and body until you die. As my years add up this is becoming a higher priority for me. A passage of Scripture that contains a promise that I am claiming for myself is, "The righteous man will flourish like the palm tree, he will grow like a cedar in Lebanon. Planted in the house of the LORD, they will flourish in the courts of our God. They will still yield fruit in old age; They shall be full of sap and very green, to declare that the LORD is upright; *He is* my rock, and there is no unrighteousness in Him" (Psalm 92:12-15).

It is like the prayer; "And even when I am old and gray, O God, do not forsake me, until I declare Your strength to this generation, Your power to all who are to come" (Psalm 71:18). This has been my purpose in writing this book. I want to pass along to the next generation some of the valuable lessons that I have learned along my journey. These lessons have become very dear to me.

This Section contains reminders of basic disciplines or activities that need to be built into life if you expect to finish well. Start them when you are young and keep them going as you mature. With all that demands our attention or distracts us we must not drop our guard; we must not neglect the basics or we will not finish well.

Chapter 10

Life-long Learning in The Word

Jesus ended His Sermon on the Mount with the well-known contrast between the wise and foolish builders. The main point is the importance of building on the foundation of the rock. The teaching of the New Testament makes clear that knowing and trusting Jesus Christ is the foundation of our faith. He is the rock. But He is also teaching about the importance of making application of the Word of God when He says, "everyone who hears these words of Mine and acts on them" (Matthew 7:24-26). Sometimes I think we understate the importance of this emphasis on *doing* because we don't want to leave the impression that salvation is based on works. It is true that you cannot work your way to heaven no matter how much you do, but long-haul obedience requires building long-haul habits of *doing* obedience that last for a lifetime (Ephesians 2:10).

The first of these long-haul disciplines is studying and applying the Word of God. You never finish with these essential activities of hearing and doing. During the last few years as I have been less active, I have found time to re-examine certain passages of Scripture and doctrines of the faith. It has allowed me to reaffirm what I have taught in the past but also explore thoughts that have been on the back burner because of time pressure. It has allowed me to sharpen biblical study tools and rekindle my passion for the Word and make sure it still burns. One of my mottos is to be a "be a life-long learner" but I also want to be a "life-long doer" of the Word. To end well you need to start well and stay on the path until you meet the Savior face to face. Learn to feed on the sweet taste of hearing and doing God's Word (Psalm 19:10; 119:103). Remember Jesus' words by the well in Samaria, "My food is to do the will of Him who sent Me and to accomplish His work" (John 4:34). Obedience to God's Word is never out of style for the believer who desires to end well.

The Importance of Studying the Bible

Let's review some basics about studying the Bible that every believer needs to know. Every Christian should be equipped to do solid Bible study. This will help you to better discern truth about God and to grow personal convictions to speak to others.

First, we should remember that truth is knowable. We live in a day of postmodern pluralism that says everyone's opinion or belief is private and only valid for them. The existence of universal truth is denied and if it did exist would be unknowable. But as believers in the Creator-God who has spoken through His Son, Jesus Christ, and in the Scriptures, (Hebrew 1:1-2) we believe that God's revelation in the Bible is trustworthy, true and knowable (2 Timothy 3:16). We should speak with confident boldness, yet with humility and gentleness, to those who have lost hope and are confused by hearing many conflicting opinions. We must faithfully point people to the God of the Bible and the truth that He has revealed.

D. A. Carson reminds us in his book, *The Gagging of God: Christianity Confronts Pluralism,* (Grand Rapids, Zondervan, 1996) that pluralism tries to force changes in hermeneutics (how to study). You must be aware of this dangerous trend today that shifts the authority away from the text to the one reading the text. You must continue to place yourself under the authority of the Scriptures in all that you do.

Second, you should keep a balance between biblical theology and systematic theology. They should inform and guard each other and should not be done in isolation. Biblical theology asks questions of the meaning of the text. Systematic theology asks summary questions like, "What is God?" If systematic theology only picks verses from Scripture to prove or support a point, but has not done the work of biblical theology that accurately exegetes the text, it will abuse and misuse the Bible and build upon an invalid foundation. You need to be diligent to do good accurate work in both your biblical theology and your systematic theology.

Let me outline a method of interpreting the Bible (using the methods of biblical theology) that I have used for over 45 years. I learned this from Dr. Walter C. Kaiser, Jr., to whom I am indebted for helping me learn how to approach Scripture. Kaiser served as academic dean and Vice President of Education and professor at Trinity Evangelical Divinity School and later as President of Gordon-Conwell Seminary. The hermeneutical method he taught was simple and easy to use. It has helped me immensely and I am very grateful for his impact on my ministry. I can still hear him admonishing the class with one of his frequent statements, "Keep your finger on the text." Here is a summary of that method.

How to Study the Bible

The three tasks of Bible study are to find:

1. ***The Meaning***
2. ***The Principle***
3. ***The Application***

1. The Meaning

There is only one meaning of a biblical text. It is the intended meaning of the author for those he was addressing. The five tools that we use for finding the meaning of the text are:

1. ***Historical Setting***
2. ***Main Idea***
3. ***Context***
4. ***Words and Sentences***
5. ***Harmony with Other Scriptures***

2. The Principle

The principle is the biblical truth stated in a simple statement that bridges the years from "then" (when the author wrote) to "now" (the present day). Other terms to describe this are: lesson, teaching, significance, and implication.

3. The Application

Personal application is taking biblical truth, making it yours and acting upon it.

I would add that we should stick to a literal interpretation of Scripture unless the author makes it clear that a metaphor or allegory is in view. There are many examples in Church history when using an allegorical interpretation got the Church off track. When dealing with a hard text or something difficult to understand (or accept) it can be tempting to use allegory. Stick to the plain and most obvious meaning of the text and let it speak. God speaks through His Word and sometimes that is uncomfortable. Be a workman that is not ashamed but accurately

Chapter 11

Life-long Learning to Pray Without Ceasing

Luke records for us the sweet relational atmosphere of God's peace among the believers in the early church in Acts Chapter 2. He describes how they "kept feeling a sense of awe," (verse 43) as they observed the Holy Spirit at work. They responded by demonstrating practical love in the generous sharing of material possessions, and a visible commitment to fellowship, as they gathered for worship. Love was overflowing within the community of believers. "Behold, how good and how pleasant it is for brothers to dwell together in unity" (Psalm 133:1).

We must not overlook the emphasis that Luke put on the focused corporate activity in the Word and prayer. "They were continually devoting themselves to the apostles' teaching and to prayer," (Acts 2:42). Is this common in most churches today?

It is this connection between the practice of devoting time to the Word and prayer that best defines the dynamic of their faith in action resulting in their relational peace. I have selected prayer as the second life-long habit to practice for finishing well.

Praying Together

You have probably heard the often repeated cliché, "the family that prays together, stays together." Not a bad catchphrase. It does remind us that praying together makes a very real positive difference in any relationship. At the core, prayer is believing 1) that God exists, 2) that He is present, and 3) that He hears and has promised to answer those who seek Him and cry out to Him in prayer (Hebrews 11:6). When I was doing marriage counseling, I often asked the question, "Do you pray together?" The most common answer was, "No, not really, or only at meals."

Beverly and I practice praying together each night as we go to bed. We take turns leading; she prays on even numbered days and I on odd. We find that we each voice aloud to God content where we agree as we come to the throne of grace. It also helps us cultivate common themes that our hearts share. It brings us together. Praying together is a good spiritual means that grows our relationship with each other as well as with God.

We do repeat many of the same requests. I think that Jesus' teaching of the widow woman who kept coming with her request before the unjust judge is a good reminder that we ought to pray and not to lose heart (Luke 18:1-8). Jesus' point was teaching that God is greater than the unjust judge in this parable and He will faithfully respond to your requests even when waiting is hard.

The Purposes of Prayer

Prayer is an important part of a dynamic relationship between God and His family. He speaks to you through His word and you speak to Him in prayer. Prayer is not about getting stuff from God; it is about developing an abiding-in-Christ relationship that God desires to have with us. He asked a penetrating question at the end of the passage:, "However, when the Son of Man comes, will He find faith on the earth?" (Luke 18:8). There is some question if Jesus was speaking of "the faith" as in the biblical doctrine of salvation or if He was referring to the dynamic of faith as exercised in prayer. I think the context of the passage may point to the lack of the practice of prayer before Christ's return.

The Bible is replete with instruction about the importance of prayer. God's will for us is clearly to continue the diligent practice of prayer, praise, thanksgiving, and making requests. "Pray without ceasing; in everything give thanks; for this is God's will for you in Christ Jesus (1 Thessalonians 5:17-18). It is also an important safeguard during spiritually dangerous times. "With all prayer and petition pray at all times in the Spirit, and with this in view, be on the alert with all perseverance and petition for all the saints" (Ephesians 6:18). Peter adds, "…casting all your anxiety on Him, because He cares for you. Be of sober spirit, be on the alert. Your adversary, the devil, prowls around like a roaring lion, seeking someone to devour. But resist him, firm in your faith" (1 Peter 5:7-9).

Another important element of prayer is the regular confession of sin (1 John 1:9). This demonstrates another link connecting the work of the Holy Spirit as He uses the sharp and penetrating nature of the Word of God and stimulates your response of faith in prayer (Hebrews 4:12). The writer reminds us that, "there is no creature hidden from His sight, but all things are open and laid bare to the eyes of Him with whom we have to do" (verse 3).

When you ignore sin and try to pretend it does not exist in your life, spiritual growth is stunted, and carnality grows. This almost always results in relational breakdown and a reduction of relational peace. The writer of Hebrews goes on to link the lack of spiritual maturity to a poor diet of the word of God (Hebrews 5:13-6:1). Peter says that we are to be "like newborn babies" and, "long for the pure milk of the Word, so that by it you may grow in respect to salvation" (1 Peter 2:2). We can conclude, therefore, that faith is both birthed and grows as we study God's Word (Romans 10:17). God works in us and speaks to us by His Spirit through His Word.

In the upper room teaching to the disciples, Jesus clearly links prayer and the application of the Word to abiding in fellowship with God (John 14-16). Also notice in the following strategic passage of instruction on living out the faith in relational peace and how Paul stressed the role of the Word of God for this quality of godly relational life.

Paul added, "...put on a heart of compassion, kindness, humility, gentleness and patience, bearing with one another, and forgiving each other, whoever has a complaint against anyone; just as the Lord forgave you, so also should you. Beyond all these things put on love, which is the perfect bond of unity. Let the peace of Christ rule in your hearts, to which indeed you were called in one body; and be thankful, Let the word of Christ richly dwell within you..." (Colossians 3:12-16).

Psalm 119:9-11 instructs the young person that the Word of God protects from the pathway of sin and therefore is worth treasuring. Later this guidance theme is repeated, "Your Word is a lamp to my feet and a light to my path" (verse 105) and "Those who love Your law have great peace, and nothing causes them to stumble" (verse 165). God's Word becomes sweeter as your fellowship with God deepens and is beautifully stated in these words, "How sweet are Your words to my taste! Yes, sweeter than honey to my mouth" (verse 103)! Each line of this prayer reminds the believer that these expressions model loving communication in a close relationship with the living God. He speaks to you through His word and you speak to Him through prayer. It is a relationship that operates in the sphere of faith and the Spirit. The more you practice tuning your ear to hear God speak in His Word and train your tongue to speak in prayer the more faith grows.

In times of spiritual battle, faith, prayer, and the Word again connect to form a strategy for your protection. The evil one often strikes when he sees vulnerability in your relationships. Remember, the Apostle Paul was writing the congregation at Corinth. They were experiencing relational struggle. He wrote to them about joining his strategy for the battle as having "the weapons of righteousness for the right hand and the left" (2 Corinthians 6:7). He develops this imagery in his letter regarding spiritual warfare to those at Ephesus, by explaining what is in his mind for the left hand, "taking up the shield of faith with which you will be able to extinguish all the flaming arrows of the evil one," and the right hand used for wielding, "the sword of the Spirit, which is the Word of God" (Ephesus 6:16-17).

Chapter 12

Life-long Witness

The Great Commission that Jesus gave to the disciples remains the task of the Church (Matthew 28:18-20). I want to be found by Jesus, at His coming or at my death, active in specific ways cooperating with Him as He builds His Church and in making disciples. Each believer should be asking how they can pray, go, support, teach, and give a word of witness more effectively. You and I are called to bear witness to the truth of the good news of God's love and grace that is wrapped up in Jesus' atoning sacrifice, His resurrection, and soon return.

Stress as a Starting Point for the Gospel

A few years ago I was asked to do some seminars for a group of thirteen ethnic church leaders located in Oslo, Norway. These churches were immigrant peoples from different African and Asian nations. The first time I met with them I shared the stress cycle and we talked a lot about understanding culture and the stress that comes from moving from one culture into another and how to thrive as displaced people. The Bible has a lot to say about living as aliens and all believers are to consider themselves as citizens of heaven. The second invitation came from this group about a year later and this time the request was to help them communicate the gospel to individuals from other cultural groups. Cross-cultural communication is what the mission mandate is all about, but cross-cultural witness is not an easy task. I took them back to the Stress Cycle and tried to help them see how one of the best ways to connect with people from any culture is to help them understand their stress experiences. Much of what I have shared in this book can be used in helping those from other cultural backgrounds. Ideal witness is not about just dumping a load of information, but rather cultivating relationships where we can open a more fully-orbed dialogue with people and share content as God opens doors of opportunity. The key is to be ready when that door opens.

I have taught many approaches to doing witnessing over the years. I have used the "Four Spiritual Laws" pioneered by Bill Bright, "Steps to Peace with God" from the Billy Graham Association, and Evangelism Explosion ("EE") as taught by D. James Kennedy. I have also cooperated with training people with the "Road to Emmaus" materials and promoted the use of inductive Bible studies to share the Gospel message. God has used all these methods.

Some methods, like EE, demand a lot of memorization and others can seem somewhat abrupt and less helpful in cross-cultural witness. Another difficulty I have discovered is that as western culture has become less committed to a biblical worldview, you cannot assume that a person to whom you are speaking has any grasp of general Bible knowledge.

Rather than choose one of these approaches to teach in Oslo, I set out to present something that would help them communicate a more robust content about God and would be both flexible and scalable. Because they wanted to share with people from other cultural backgrounds, they would not be able to assume how much each person knew about the God of the Bible. Many of the people they would encounter did not have a biblical worldview or basic exposure to the biblical narrative.

A plan was needed to lay a solid foundation of theology that could flesh out their witness. Such a plan would need to be flexible enough to insert Scriptural truth content about God into a continuing conversation over time. My goal was to provide a mental map that could be easily recalled by using memory hooks to help those desiring to share their faith. This would help boost their confidence to speak to others about some of the deeper thoughts of who God is, why we serve Him (witness), and explain the gospel that He provides through Christ.

This seminar turned into the book *God Talk: 13 Things Everybody Needs to Know About God.* I explain in the Addendum how five of these thirteen core doctrines provide the theological foundation of the strategy for managing personal stress.

Being prepared to help a person understand their stress and give a testimony how God has helped you in your times of stress can open doors for witnessing. Introduce them to the God who cares about them with love and grace.

Staying ready and active in speaking a witness of God's grace and peace is one of the essentials in doing life for the long-haul and finishing well.

Chapter 13

Life-long Accountability for The Glory of God

When a person neglects the safeguards that accountability partnerships provide, they may be headed for real trouble. If you take seriously that the adversary is doing his best to destroy your relationships, then you will cultivate life-long relationships of accountability. The Apostle Peter warned about this powerful enemy (1 Peter 5:8). He often takes advantage of unexpected stressful events to launch a blindside attack. It is during these times of reacting to stress that you are probably the most vulnerable. When your defenses are down it is easy to react in the flesh at a weak moment and allow him to do some painful damage.

The writer of the book of Hebrews develops a series of warnings that are all good safeguards to building a life of faith. A valuable exercise would be to do a study through that book with another person asking the question, "How can you and I partner to keep these warnings in view?"

A great summary of this concept of accountability teaching is, "Let us hold fast the confession of our hope without wavering, for He who promised is faithful; and let us consider how to stimulate one another to love and good deeds, not forsaking our own assembling together..." (Hebrews 10:23 25a).

This is not just about membership and attendance at a local church (although that may be a good starting point); it is about pursuing accountability relationships where you seriously "consider how to stimulate" each other to stay faithful and on track.

I have worked in counseling with many Christian workers who have not maintained accountability relationships and have fallen into sin that sidelined their effectiveness in ministry. Practicing an authentic, honest and transparent accountability partnership could have made a real difference to safeguard them from significant pain. Giving a few significant fellow believers permission to ask you anything is a great safeguard and a key to life-long accountability.

Chapter 14

Life-long Physical Disciplines

A book on stress would not be complete without addressing some mention of the physical aspects. Often in the past when speaking on stress I would make a few comments about pertaining to "Try Harder" (number 5 on the Stress Cycle) but not dig down. I would say something to the effect of, "Trying harder can be a conscious attempt to control the next thing on the agenda, or it can be a point where some people give up and disengage. It can also represent the physiological component and remind you that it is the body's way of trying to help you get back in control of your world." While these observations are true, they were pretty superficial. I would usually say a few words about the many stress hormones that have been discovered that can influence your health. I failed, however, to give much practical information on this subject as I did not feel qualified to venture into the biological sciences and domain of medicine more than to say, "The medical community generally agrees that every illness has a stress component."

The Impact of Health on Stress

During the past several years I have become more interested in researching health issues and the role played by stress. As I age, I want to stay healthy and productive for as long as possible. I want to stay useful. In my book, *In Whatever State I Am: Learning the Lessons of Contentment,* I tell the story of having a five-way bypass heart surgery while writing and trying to live by the lessons I was writing about. As I write today, I have lived with diagnosed heart disease for nearly 30 years, and it has been fifteen years since my surgery. Stress has played a significant role in my journey to this point. As I look forward to the next season in my life, I want to be a good steward of the years that God gives me. Since I have lived with significant heart disease for roughly half of my adult life, I need to better understand this subject and I want to pass along some of what I am learning.

The world of biological medicine is in a period of transition. Many of those who practice medicine are finding this a little awkward and uncomfortable while others are embracing and adapting. Change is not easy and it feels safer to stick to what was taught earlier. The speed of new information in the bio-science world can make your head spin. But common beliefs and practices are slow to change.

When I had my first heart episode 29 years ago, I was treated with an angioplasty procedure (a balloon placed in the artery and expanded) which probably saved my life as I had a complete blockage of the anterior artery that is called "the widow maker." I am grateful for that medical intervention. At that time, however, I received and followed the advice given me by the doctors and the hospital staff to practice a low fat, high carbohydrate diet, which I dutifully did. What current research is discovering is that was counterproductive misinformation and probably did more harm than good. Old habits are difficult to change, even among professionals who are expected to be up to date on the latest research. As I talk with medical people, I find many are still living and practicing by the old dietary formula from years ago. My interest in the research has also been driven by what I am observing across the landscape of my friends and the general population with deteriorating health, obesity, heart disease, dementia, cancer, type 2 diabetes, arthritis and autoimmune disease. I would rather learn and change than succumb to this rising tide of illness. The research is showing that stress is a significant component in each of the maladies just listed.

I had to ask myself, "What connections are there between my stress, my diet, and my personal health issues?" My pursuit has led me to make significant changes in my own lifestyle. I started about five years ago and have lost close to fifty pounds. I wish I had known some of this information earlier in life. Without getting too far into the weeds I will try to share some thoughts.

My recommendations are simple. Get a second opinion. Keep learning. Read widely. Search the literature. At least read the summaries of the research if not the full studies of what is being published. Pay particular attention to the last ten years of material. There is a lot of information out there and not all of it is trustworthy. If you can't do it yourself, find some trusted voices who can interpret the data for you. I will provide some names that have been helpful to me in the Addendum to help you get started.

Chronic Stress

I mentioned in Chapter 1 that stress can be chronic or acute. Chronic stress (over time) is the most damaging to your health. Periods of rest are therefore important. God's Word teaches some good principles regarding the importance of sleep, and periodic rest. I am not suggesting that believers during the Church Age keep Jewish laws pertaining to rest; however, we can learn important principles from these Old Testament practices. The wise person will build times of rest into their life. Learning to take short breaks, walks, power naps, times of prayer, meditation on Scripture, or even a few moments of deep breathing are great ways to send a message to the body to relax and rest. There is much new research being published about the relationship between sleep and stress, and the importance of having a full night's sleep and its role in staying healthy, especially as one gets older.

The balance between good stress and bad stress is crucial to keep in mind. Rest and stress need to be in a healthy balance, and that must be intentionally managed. Too much stress or too much rest can be out of balance. The appropriate amount of each will depend on many factors and is very personal.

Chronic stress can damage the body through the overproduction of stress hormones over time. The hypothalamus gland sets off an alarm system that triggers both nerves and hormones. This alert system produces a surge of stress hormones that include adrenaline and cortisol (over fifty have been identified). God designed this to function for short bursts of time to help us in dangerous situations. When you live with the alert system constantly switched on, you begin to have some negative and eventually dangerous breakdowns in the systems of the body. Adrenaline increases your heart rate and elevates your blood pressure. Cortisol, another primary stress hormone, increases sugars (glucose) in the bloodstream, and curbs or alters the immune system, as well as a host of other responses including the digestive system, mood control, and fear. Insulin is another crucial stress hormone that regulates the proper amount of sugar in the blood. It also serves as the gatekeeper for glucose into the cells to burn or to store as fat. Insulin resistance, or metabolic syndrome, is a condition when the body is stressed and overwhelmed by a long-term diet high in sugar. The regulation of sugar in the blood is a high priority to maintain life. Eating a high carbohydrate diet that is too high in sugar over-stresses this important system over time. Research is showing that this is the primary cause of inflammation which appears to be a major primary causal factor in almost every major disease including the heart, brain, fatty liver, arthritis, weight gain, and the list goes on.

We have known for years that when under stress people tend to seek out "comfort food" which usually involves eating more sugar, which triggers the pleasure center of the brain. For many this becomes a vicious downward cycle that negatively affects emotional moods even more. Many experts today now opine that a high carbohydrate diet of highly processed foods (that include processed seed oils and ingredients like high fructose corn syrup) can change your brain chemistry and cause damage that leads to a host of health issues.

You can train your body, however, to burn fat rather than sugar. That is a cornerstone of a number of new popular diets, including ketogenic, paleo, and carnivore diets. What I was told over a quarter of a century ago was to eat a low-fat diet but today there is a growing body of evidence that a diet high in fat and low in carbohydrates is far superior. In addition to heart health, new research and clinical practice is showing this is true of many other common maladies. This includes Alzheimer's disease and new evidence is showing that it can be either slowed or even reversed. So be careful who you listen to. It pays to be a discerning consumer of information.

Benefits of Fasting

Another connection between stress and food is fasting. Fasting is good stress that promotes healing and health. Fasting has been practiced as a component in religion for centuries but there is a mountain of new research evidence that shows practicing intermittent fasting, or time restricted feeding, can reverse metabolic syndrome. Not only is this proving to be a key to successful weight loss, but it is also demonstrating a reduction of inflammation in various parts of the body.

Again, fasting is a good stress and can be used along with exercise (another form of good stress) to promote autophagy (the self-eating of damaged cells). It is cheap and available to everyone. Autophagy is the body's process of cleaning out old, damaged cells so that new ones can grow and take their place. Good stress is necessary for this cleaning process, and fasting will trigger it. Periodic cleanup of debris is important. Damaged and worn outworn-out cells accumulate and need to be reprocessed or replaced. A generation ago medical schools taught that brain cells could not regenerate. Today, however, new discoveries in the plasticity of the brain are showing both regeneration and rewiring do take place.

Other Health Considerations

Another good stress for the body is heat and cold. The Finns and other Scandinavians have been using the sauna and immersing themselves in cold water for centuries to improve their health.

Physical exercises such as jogging and weight training are also good examples of putting the body under stress to improve metabolic function. These are all good examples of using stress to improve the metabolism.

To sum up, I would encourage you to consider taking some new steps. Use the IAR approach from Chapter 1 (Identify – Act – Rest). Identify or investigate changes that are appropriate for you, make a plan and then implement it by taking action. Then, rest in the Lord as you walk with Him for His glory and your Shalom (peace and health). He designed the human body, and He is the God of peace and soul rest.

Doing Life for The Long-Haul and Finishing Well

Recently at church the pastor was lamenting about several of his friends in ministry that have gotten sidetracked and are not finishing well. It was evident that the pastor was deeply moved by these unnamed individuals who had stumbled in the final stretch of life. He was tasteful in how he shared, but it is sobering when someone actually says it out loud. The Bible is full of warnings to stay the course and finish the race. The Apostle Paul repeatedly reflects in the Pastoral Epistles (written late in his life and near the end of his ministry) on finishing the race that God had called him to run and giving instruction to the younger men (Timothy and Titus) on how to stay on track. These last 5 chapters were an attempt to describe activities that make a difference for the long-haul and for finishing well. The early chapters focused more on how stress can blindside us to get us off course and damage our key relationships. The reasons people leave the ministry are varied but often can be traced back to the big three desires of the world: "the lust of the flesh, the lust of the eyes and the boastful pride of life" (1 John 2:16). I would venture a guess that more leave the ministry today due to stress related relational issues than any other single issue.

I encourage you to consider building a personal plan to help keep you on track so that stress does not derail you on the long-haul. May God give you wisdom and discernment.

Part of my personal game plan is to present my body to God each day. This concept is taught by Paul in Romans Chapters 6, 8 and 12. I need to be reminded daily that God has a claim on my body, "I have been bought with a price" - I belong to Him (1 Corinthians 6:10-20). Remember that the Apostle wrote these words to the carnal and relationally divided Corinthian church. As they needed to be reminded of this concept so does the Church today. Here are a few things that every believer should keep in mind.

1. Presenting your physical body to God is a reasonable response to His grace and mercy. It is not a work that brings merit but a command to be obeyed that affords benefits. It is a grace response that pleases

God. It is an act of worship. The Apostle says it like this, "by the mercies of God present your bodies as a living and holy sacrifice, acceptable to God, which is your spiritual service of worship" (Romans 12:1).

2. This action is a logical application of the teaching in Romans Chapter 6 and 8 where Paul lays down the foundations for victorious living in Christ. Based upon the fact of the believer's union with Christ in His death and resurrection we are to live based on the reality of that truth. We are to "consider" it to be true and then "present" ourselves to Him (Romans 6:11-13). It helps me to do this every day. I need the reminder that "walking according to the Spirit" is a dynamic that starts with acknowledging that He is "in charge" and that I am not free to do with my body whatever I want. I cannot allow my body to set the agenda for the day. Paul's testimony was, "I discipline my body and make it my slave" (1 Corinthians 9:27). Paul's practice of self-disciple was only possible as he personally applied what he was teaching. He understood that consistently presenting his body to God as an act of worship was essential in allowing the Holy Spirit to produce His fruit (Galatians 5:22-24).

3. Paul follows this instruction about presenting our bodies to God with two commands. The first is a negative present tense imperative which means to stop "conforming to this world" (Romans 12:2). I need to remind myself each day that I must operate as a citizen of heaven under His leadership and not just "fit in" acting like everyone around me. Then Paul gives a last command to "be transformed by the renewing of your mind" followed by a purpose clause "so that you may prove" or demonstrate with your life that God's way is best. We do this by abiding in Christ and in His Word (John 15:4-5, 7).

My practice is to pray something like this each day. "I present my body to You Lord as an act of worship in obedience to Your Word. I want You to dwell in my body as Your temple. I desire to live today in Your presence and to be at Your disposal for service today." The rest of Romans spells out what that kind of service should look like.

Next, I break this overall commitment into four specific component parts of my body that illustrate who I am. These four are: Head – Heart – Hands – Feet. I start with my head and move toward my feet. The head and heart represent my inner man. The hands and feet remind me of the outer man - my going and doing. These are the "what" and "where" issues of the day. Many Scripture passages that use this language often come to mind as I pray through this commitment. I will list just a few passages.

- **Head:** Psalm 119:9,11; Psalm 37:5
- **Heart:** Psalm 37:1, 7-8; Proverbs 4:23; Matthew 22:37-39; 1 John 3:18-22
- **Hands:** Psalm 90:17
- **Feet:** Psalm 119:105; Psalm 37:5, 23; Proverbs 3:5-6; James 4:13-17

I retrace back from my feet back to my head and pause at each to reflect and pray that the Lord work in my life. I am reminded that I need the Lord's direction in every area. I desire to practice the "Lordship of Christ" in everything as the day unfolds.

Section IV
Stories that Illustrate

Solomon: A Wise but Foolish Man

Solomon, the young newly anointed king over Israel, when given the opportunity to make a request of God, asked for understanding and discernment (1 Kings 3:5-14). The Scripture narrative tells us that even though King David was a man after God's own heart he was not allowed to build what would have been his crowning achievement – a temple for God. The reason given was that he had been a man of war and conflict. Rather, God promised to give David a son, "Behold, a son shall be born to you, who shall be a man of rest; and I will give him rest from all his enemies on every side; for his name shall be Solomon, and I will give peace and quiet to Israel in his days" (1 Chronicles 22:8-9). Notice the cluster of words used here; rest, peace, and quiet – something we all long for in our relationships. Too often, however, we experience our share of strife and relational conflict.

Solomon's name is a play on words with the Hebrew word *shalom* meaning peace. This son of David, whom God named, would have the honor of building a Temple that would symbolize God's dwelling among His people Israel. It would be a place to meet and fellowship with God in prayer and worship. This "son of peace" would be granted a generation of political peace with the surrounding nations. We also know from the New Testament genealogy of Jesus that this promise to David included his being part of the human line from Abraham all the way to the promised Messiah, the Prince of Peace, who would sit upon the throne of David. This promise is what biblical scholars call the Davidic Covenant. Solomon is not the final fulfillment but a foreshadowing of the One who would bring ultimate peace (Ephesians 2:13-14; Revelation 20:4-6).

The biblical writers celebrate Solomon's great successes. God's blessing was clearly upon him as a leader but they also record that he had a divided heart. He loved the Lord but there were gaping holes of inconsistency in his life. Early in his reign God had appeared to him in a dream and said, "Ask what you wish me to give you." His request pleased God and he was blessed with not only great wisdom but also wealth, fame, and success. Solomon's written contribution to the Scriptures make up a large portion of what is known as the wisdom literature of the Hebrew Bible. But his story is also a sad one and filled with irony because even though he reached a pinnacle of success he failed to walk in the way of the wisdom that he knew. He failed to put into practice his own counsel. He was not obedient to the calling of God on his life to walk in the light. His testimony in the book of Ecclesiastes reads like the reflections of a grumpy old man; "I have seen all the things that are done under the sun; all of them are meaningless, a chasing after the wind" (Ecclesiastes 1:14). God had given him a pivotal conditional promise, "if you keep my My ways then..." (v14). It is interesting that his father David had given him a very similar charge, "Be strong, therefore, and show yourself a man. And keep the charge of the LORD your God, to walk in His ways..." (1 Kings 2:2-3).

The key to relational peace is the consistent application or practice of the truth found in the Scriptures. Daily consistent obedience to our Lord over time brings great dividends to our relationships.

God was gracious to Solomon. During his lifetime the judgment he deserved for his sin was postponed, but the seeds of his disobedience were sown and the nation would later reap a harvest of division, strife, and broken fellowship.

Unfortunately, many families, ministry teams and churches today, like Solomon, know more truth about God's way of relational peace than they experience. Sometimes the seeds of sin have been sown for years or even generations before the harvest. Often behaviors and practices that have not been addressed are left to fester and grow. Discord and disagreements sown can reap a whirlwind of conflict and brokenness in families and churches. The warning of the Apostle Paul is true, "Do not be deceived: God cannot be mocked. A man reaps what he sows" (Galatians 6:7). Some harvests come sooner, some come later.

Two Sets of Brothers

Genesis records that there were two sets of historic brothers who went separate directions. They were Cain and Abel, and Esau and Jacob. You may already know much of their stories. The alert reader of Genesis will remember that Cain and Esau were both firstborn sons. This gave them a special standing in the family including both birthright and blessing. They were hence privileged. Both, however, walked in spiritual darkness, which led to relational conflict and estrangement. Cain saw no need for a substitutionary blood sacrifice for his sin to gain a right standing before God, but rather attempted to do worship and have fellowship with God on his own terms.

Moses, as the human writer telling this story, and his readers, would understand that he was laying a foundation in these early stories for and understanding what would become clear later. These stories come alive when seen through the lens of the books of Exodus, Leviticus, Numbers, and Deuteronomy. The New Testament perspective on the story is even more developed and we read that, "By faith Abel offered to God a better sacrifice than Cain…and though he is dead, still speaks."

The lives of Cain and Abel are examples that speak graphically about broken relationships and disobedience, as well as faith and walking in the light (Hebrews 11:4). Abel had a short life but his great faith-testimony continues to this day. Cain on the other hand suffered a long life of guilt, fear, and separation from God and family. His own family line is one of fear, violence, and revenge (Genesis 4:12-24). Cain's life and lineage is an illustration of "no rest" which resulted from a lack of faith and obedience.

Esau, like Cain, saw little value in having a spiritual birthright as firstborn. He sold this privilege to his brother Jacob for a meal of lentil stew (Genesis 25:29-34). The biblical record then goes on to highlight a life-long history of fear, distrust, and relational estrangement for Esau. His life and his lineage both picture what life with "no rest" looks like. Any life devoid of faith in God and obedience to Him will reap a similar harvest.

Jacob had a long and complicated spiritual and relational pilgrimage. Even though he was blessed by God, a careful study of his life provides vast material for a case study to illustrate how a self-centered man of personal struggle related to others with unremitting relational difficulty. Jacob did eventually come to embrace God by faith, but most of his life was not marked by walking daily in the "faith-rest" principle. His story is an amazing example of God's grace, having his name changed from Jacob the "supplanter", to Israel "a prince with God," and being given a legacy as the father of the twelve tribes of Israel. His testimony before Pharaoh as an old man is sad, to say the least, when he said, "The years of my sojourning …have been few and unpleasant" (Genesis 47:9). He had the opportunity to bear a joyous testimony of the grace, faithfulness, goodness, and the blessing of God, but rather Jacob spoke of the unhappiness and sorrow that was the fruit from of a self-willed life from trying to control people and events.

Jacob's Lifelong Struggle

Jacob's life story is a picture of struggle for control. His name means "one who grasps or supplants another". He was chosen by God, held a special place in the line of the Messiah, and was a true Old Testament believer, yet we see repeated stress, relational messes, and frustration that resulted from his control issues. When Rachel and Jacob had a conflict over Rachel's inability to have children, the Bible tells us that Rachel said, "Give me children, or I'll die" (Genesis 30:1). That was the deep cry of a heart under stress: the stress of having no control over the most important thing in her life, bearing children.

Notice in Jacob's response his own emotional stress reaction and how it put additional pressure on their deteriorating, stress-filled, marital relationship. The text says, "Jacob became angry with her and said, 'Am I in the place of God, who has kept you from having children?'" Jacob asked the right question. He put his finger on this most crucial issue of his life. Jacob had been acting like he could control the events of his life. He had been trying to take the place of God. Right from birth, Jacob had been scrapping, conniving, bargaining, and doing everything humanly possible to live his life in his own strength and under his own control.

Early in Jacob's life when he ran from his brother Esau in Genesis Chapter 28, God revealed himself to Jacob in the dream that is called Jacob's ladder. It is interesting to note how Jacob tried to make a deal with God. He made a conditional promise of commitment to God. He bargained with God to give him what he wanted. Notice the if/then nature of his commitment. "If God will" do these things for me, "then the Lord will be my God." Many of us can identify with Jacob. We too have our list of what we want God to do for us. If God will come through and give us what we want, if God will fill our wish list, then maybe we will submit and let the Lord be our God.

The story of Jacob wrestling with God is filled with lessons about control (Genesis 32). The name of the place is significant; Jabbok means "the place of emptying." Jacob was truly in a difficult spot. He could not go back to his uncle Laban who was now angry and estranged. Now Jacob was about to face his brother Esau who was coming to meet him with 400 armed men. This is the same brother whom Jacob had cheated twice and whose last words were still ringing in his ears, "I will kill my brother Jacob."

Jacob sent his family and all his possessions ahead across the brook Jabbok and he was alone and empty before God. All night he wrestled with the Angel of the Lord trying to force a blessing of protection from God. Just who prevails in this story? It seems God was forcing the issue with Jacob.

God gave Jacob two things to remind him of that all-night struggle. First, God gave him a limp that he would have for the rest of his life. God touched Jacob in the largest muscle of the body, his thigh. I believe God did this to give Jacob a lasting reminder that his own strength was not sufficient; Jacob's strength was not sovereign strength. This is a lesson that we must learn as well. Our greatest strength is not sufficient, no matter how hard we try.

Second, God gave Jacob a new name – the name Israel. What a significant name it was. The name made of two Hebrew words; God, and wrestle. What was God saying to Jacob by giving him this new name? I believe that something very significant was happening. Jacob had a reputation for wrestling for himself. I think God was saying to him, Jacob, stop wrestling with life and the events that I have put into your path. Stop wrestling with Me. Stop wrestling for yourself and let Me wrestle for you. Enthrone Me as the Sovereign Lord of all the events of your life. Acknowledge Me as your Sovereign King and submit to Me in every detail as it unfolds. Relinquish control to Me. Rest in Me and I will supply all your needs and give you joy and rest.

Jacob sacrificed much of the joy that could have been his. His life story remains one of constantly usurping God's role and trying to run his life on his own terms, seeking what he thought would bring him joy and satisfaction.

Common but Painful Life Struggles

Tom poured out his frustration as we both awkwardly toyed with our coffee cups in a local café. I had observed some troubling symptoms over the last few months, but as a young youth pastor I didn't know what to do, and I had been reluctant to ask what was happening. After all, I was only a youth pastor. I excused myself by thinking he would take the initiative when he was ready to open up. Now, in spite of his smooth and confident exterior, it all spilled out - a deteriorating relationship with his wife, financial problems, pressure at work, feeling like a failure, and a growing weight of anger and resentment.

Tom's story (like our two sets of brothers from Genesis) illustrates the kind of struggle that comes from the consequences of unmanaged personal stress. Rather than facing issues, he had escaped into his work and hobbies. Over time the tension grew into a persistent sense of defeat and failure. His doctor assured him that the lingering knot in his stomach was not physical, but that he needed to talk with someone about it before it became a medical problem. Thus our prolonged late night meeting over coffee and his blunt questions; "Pastor, where is God when I need Him? I thought He was supposed to be on my side."

I will never forget the sense of inadequacy that I felt. I didn't know what to say or what to do. I didn't have a visual roadmap to connect the dots at that time. I was ill-prepared to help my friend with his deteriorating marriage and personal life. Everything that I suggested he dismissed with, "I've done that and it didn't help." That evening I determined that I needed to become better equipped if I was going to be of any significant help to people in need.

Like Tom, many Christians are not experiencing the full measure of joy, peace, and rest that the Bible speaks about and that God desires for their lives. Many feel that they are being robbed of the pleasure of walking in intimate fellowship with God, the very thing for which we were designed. Too often believers allow stress to steal their joy.

Can you identify with Tom? Are you prepared to help someone like Tom? Can you point the way to live a satisfying, intimate, God-centered life in the midst of the turmoil that stress brings? And, for that matter, are you currently enjoying a daily walk of close fellowship with God and enjoying the fruit of a God-centered life yourself?

Pain Motivates

Robert was a prominent professional whose life had been suddenly jolted. His wife announced that she was leaving him. He came to my office to ask me what he should do to get her to change her mind. As we explored the situation together, we found that he had little awareness of how his behavior and his own stress reactions were negatively affecting his family. He had shrugged off his wife's attempts to communicate her frustration and now he faced the prospects of a very painful separation. Suddenly it seemed to him everything was out of control. Robert's stress level had reached a threshold of pain that motivated him to begin to consider how his behavior was being perceived by his wife and family. The crisis had provided an opportunity.

The Chinese character for crisis is written by combining the symbols for danger and opportunity. What a fantastic picture of stress; both danger and opportunity. Stress often feels like a crisis, but it can also lead to new opportunities for growth into the person God has designed you to be.

A Postponed Flight

A few years ago my wife Bev and I were scheduled to travel back to our home in Florida. We had finished a conference the evening before in the beautiful mountains of California. Our plan was to head back home following our well laid out plans. After waking up early, we walked to a restaurant for a leisurely breakfast. Our flight was to leave at 10:30, so we called for a taxi at about 8:30. We were informed that it would be over an hour before we could get a taxi and the airport was at least 30 minutes away. I experienced a quick flash of stress as I processed our options and the thought that we weren't going to get to the airport on time. The dispatcher then said if we were ready at that moment, she could get us a ride. We gave her our location and walked out to the parking lot to meet the taxi. Twenty minutes later the cell phone rang. The driver could not find our location, a second stressor. The taxi did eventually find us and we were off to the airport.

Since it was foggy, we asked at the check-in counter if the flight would be on time. "No problem," we were told. "Your plane is on its way here right now." An hour later there was an announcement. It was too foggy for the plane to land and our flight had been cancelled. Another stressor. After waiting in line for half an hour with 50 other passengers, we were booked on a flight that left three hours later. We landed at the airport in Los Angeles ten minutes too late to catch our next plane. The next available flight would not leave for ten hours. This meant waiting to take the "red eye" (the night flight) home, or waiting until the next day.

Stress occurs when things don't go as planned. It gets more complicated when we respond incorrectly. We make plans and expect life to go according to our agenda. But life is full of interruptions, surprises, and delays to our plans and schedules. Our travel story illustrates the idea, but being delayed for 24 hours is not a big deal. It is a common experience for those who travel. If we had a very important engagement at our destination that we were missing it would have been more stressful. If a family member was in critical condition in a hospital and we were hurrying to get there, we would have felt even more stress. The details of this story were all under the providence of the sovereign God whom we were serving, but that didn't lower our experience of stress until we took action to pray and rest in Him.

Driven for Success

As James rides the bus to work he contemplates what his boss will say to him at his annual performance review. It has been a good year. James is sure he will receive a good report and a substantial raise in pay. The stated corporate values of the company are to reward those who work hard. These resonate with his values and James has high expectations of what will happen today. After all, he has been putting an enormous amount of energy into trying to control the events at work and prove he is a successful leader. The day begins with anticipation and expectations of good things to come.

James' boss frowns as he opens the large manila folder holding the personnel records. As he reads the summary evaluation James is stunned. He cannot believe that he is not being appreciated for his hard work. Rather than being rewarded, he is being demoted to a lower position, which will mean less responsibility and a smaller salary.

James' thoughts race, but he remains silent. He says to himself, "I don't agree with how the boss is leading the company. I don't agree with his thinking, or what he is saying, but I need this job." He realizes that he has no control over the actions of the boss who has all the power and seems to be acting in a very controlling manner. James begins to feel frustrated, hurt, and angry.

As James rides the bus home that evening, he begins to have self-deprecating thoughts and feelings. Just that morning he had been anticipating the future and the opportunities that were on the horizon.

Now he is telling himself that he is worthless and will never amount to anything.

During the evening meal James is extraordinarily critical of the food his wife prepared and says unkind things to his children. Before long his stress is negatively affecting all of the relationships in the family.

James cannot sleep as he rehearses the day's events in his mind. The more he thinks, the angrier he becomes. By morning he is feeling depressed and hopeless. His head hurts. He is having chest pains. He believes he is having a heart attack. James is experiencing stress that has to do with his reactions to events that are beyond his control. Several of the most common stressors are jobs, money, and other people's behavior.

Striving for Perfection and Identity

Sandy was experiencing a great deal of stress due to the pressure she placed upon herself, believing she was responsible for the behavior of her husband and children. This is a common source of internal stress. Sandy was inflicting herself with large doses of stress because she kept rehearsing the popular myth that she could control her family's behavior. The more she reviewed her failure in her mind the more defeated she became.

Bill was a fine and dedicated physician who would go into a tailspin each time one of his patients would take a turn for the worse. When he lost a patient to death, he would berate himself and question his worth as a physician. Bill had slipped into the false but common belief that he, as a doctor, had more power and responsibility to control things than was truly humanly possible.

Bill and Sandy can remind us of our own tendency to expect more from ourselves than we can deliver. We desire to help others and would like to have the power to control each situation. This is especially true when something is really important to us. We think that we should be able to control everything around us. Like those we work with, we also bring expectations and a sense of what is ideal to everything that happens to us. The stronger one's view of what *should* happen, the stronger the sense of let down when it doesn't. We tend to set ourselves up for being let down, the stronger the expectation the stronger our stress reaction. When expectations are based upon false beliefs that are rehearsed for years, they become entrenched. None of us are exempt from struggling with our own idealistic expectations about control. This slavery to ladder thinking hinders your walk of faith and the joy of resting in Jesus.

Addendum

#1
Problem Solving in Helping Others

Identify–Act–Rest

Stress sometimes calls for problem solving. If problem solving is the best approach the question changes to, "What action can be taken to change this situation?" Problem solving can be a good solution to relieve stress and help a person think through the possible consequences of taking action. This can be a very important ministry. It is best not to tell them what to do but to help them think about what might happen if they would take a particular action. Coach a person to consider as many possible action plans as possible before deciding on one. Sometimes people develop tunnel vision and they fail to see that they have numerous options that could be taken. Don't jump too quickly to take the first action that sounds like it might work. Wisdom is choosing the right solution. A good question to ask is, "What might happen if you do this?" Or, "What are possible consequences of this choice?"

Again, resist the temptation to tell people what to do. Sometimes dependent people will try to get you to make their decisions for them. They want you to tell them what to do. You should not take the responsibility of making their decision for them; this only reinforces their dependency. It may make you feel important to give good answers or tell them what to do, but it may not help in the long run. If your suggestion doesn't work you can get caught in an endless round of advice giving and failed attempts at change. They will only blame you for the failure, seeing themselves as victims of your bad advice. Watch out for individuals who are stuck in a passive kind of anger who need someone to blame more than they desire to solve the problem.

Problem-solving approaches can be effective in many cases, but you need the wisdom of the Holy Spirit when using them. First help the person clarify if problem solving is appropriate. Then encourage them to identify what power they have and coach them to make those changes. Examples might include things like learning some new organizing or time management skills.

An Eight Step Problem-Solving Approach

Identify–Act–Rest

Step 1. Identify what needs to change. Pray and ask God for direction. What is the ideal? What has gone wrong? What will happen if no change is made? How will this change affect others?

Step 2. Identify any anticipated resistance. Who and what will resist making a change? What is holding the person back? What are the costs of making this change?

Step 3. Identify the resources needed to make the change. What resources are available (social programs, money, people, pastors, friends, etc)?

Step 4. Identify the steps needed to implement the change. How does the person get from here (where they are) to there (where they want to be)?

Step 5. Act in the strength God provides. When should the person take the action? How should the action be done?

Step 6. Assess and evaluate. What worked? What didn't?

Step 7. Adjust and persist in taking additional action steps.

Step 8. Celebrate the results, thank God and rest in God's providence.

#2
Toward a Better Understanding of the Role of Distress and The Implications for Evangelism

(Excerpts from God Talk: 13 Things Everybody Needs to Know About God)

When you encounter people in distress, your first response is usually to do what you can to provide relief. This is good, noble and biblical, but your thinking about distress probably needs to be stretched. Witnessing or speaking about "God talk" during times of distress can be risky, yet richly rewarding. Discomfort, pain and suffering are universal, but uniquely personal, ranging from the minor irritant to painful paralysis. Relevant God talk must be sensitive to the individual's experience and have a good theology of distress. Medical literature speaks about distress in a technical way. It is referred to as a negative state of failure to cope with stress (a maladaptive response that diminishes functioning) or to the heightened emotional reaction caused by a stressful event (a stressor). This may be true and helpful for the academic, but it leaves God out of the picture. What does distress have to do with God? What is God doing in this uncomfortable situation? To dialogue with a person about these questions you must start with a better understanding of what the Bible teaches about distress. The word *distress* is used broadly in both Old and New Testaments and deserves careful attention. The English word distress is found only 83 times, but when we search the nearly 20 Greek and Hebrew words associated with it, the use jumps to over 450 times. If the search is expanded to include related words (like sorrow) we discover a vast subject that demands our study.

The biblical writers speak about distress in three general categories. First, external events that are distressful which are often descriptions of people being in circumstances of trouble or "straits" of some kind. Second, the emotional feelings of distress that people experience internally. Third, the distress caused by God's hand of judgment, sometimes past and sometimes pointing to a future time of great trouble or tribulation that is predicted to come upon the world that will produce great distress upon mankind.

A few examples might be helpful. Jacob felt emotional distress due to having conflict with others and from having an encounter with God (Genesis 28:17; 32:7; 35:3). David experienced emotional distress during a stressful situation and "found strength in the Lord his God" (1 Samuel 30:6). The Psalms provide 17 specific examples of distress (where the word *distress* is used, Psalm 4:1; 18:6; 25:17; 31:9; 35:26; 59:16; 66:14; 69:17; 71:20; 102:2; 106:44; 107:6, 13, 19, 28; 116:3; 118:5). Six are prayers that cry out for relief from distress; ten are expressions of worship, testimony or thanksgiving for having received relief from distress. Almost half are attributed to David.

In Moses' sermon in Deuteronomy, he prophesied that God would bring distress upon the covenant people Israel for their disobedience and then foretold how he He would use it to bring them to repentance (Deuteronomy 4:27-31; 28:45-68). Moses also told how God used distress to harden the heart of Pharaoh when the Israelites were brought out of Egypt (Deuteronomy 6:22).

The book of Judges records a pattern of repeated cycles demonstrating God's use of distress to bring the people to a point of repentance from sin and to cry out to God for relief (Judges 2:15; 10:9,14). In the book of Ruth, Naomi assumes God's hand of judgment is upon her when her husband and two sons die in Moab and she says, "Call me Mara, because the Almighty has made my life very bitter" and "The Lord has afflicted me; the Almighty has brought misfortune upon me" (Ruth 1:13; 20-21). In 1 Samuel we discover a number of examples of the writer contrasting godly and ungodly reactions to distress (1 Samuel 1:10; 2:32; 10:19; 15:10-11; 22:2; 26:24; 30:6; 28:15). Hannah, in distress, poured out her heart to God in prayer. The word *distress* is used in the prophecy regarding the coming judgment on Eli's family. When God accused the people of rejecting His leadership by demanding a king, God described Himself as the One "who saves you out of all your calamities and distresses." The text says Samuel was distressed when God disclosed to him, "I am grieved that I have made Saul king" and "he cried out to the Lord all that night." The writer recorded that those who were distressed joined David, God's anointed future king.

David expressed hope in God's deliverance and found strength in the Lord when experiencing distress in contrast to Saul when he was approaching the end of his life and expressed the words, "I am in great distress." Amnon worked himself into a state of emotional distress succumbing to the temptation of lust and sexual sin. This is contrasted with David rejoicing in God's deliverance and looking to God's mercy even when he sinned by counting the fighting men (2 Samuel 13:2; 22:17-20; 24:14). The concept of distress permeates the writings of the prophets. Typically it is viewed as caused by God's hand of judgment (Judges 2:15; 10:9,14; Ruth 1:13; 20-21; 1 Samuel 1:10; 2:32; 10:19; 15:10-11; 22:2; 26:24;

30:6; 28:15; 2 Samuel 13:2; 2 Samuel 22:17-20; 24:14) and frequently involved opposing armies to punish Israel, Judah or other nations for their sin (Isaiah 5:30; Jeremiah 19:9). In Haggai chapter Chapter 1 the Lord's message to the post-exile people makes it clear that it is God's action that brought economic difficulty, poor harvests and monetary inflation (all forms of distress) to the people.

#3
Practical Insights and Guidelines for Stress Management

1. Be a lifelong learner without being self-absorbed or defensive. Defensive people rarely grow because they are closed to new ideas. They are too busy defending themselves or their ideas to hear anything new. Ask God to help you to be open, not only to new things, but specifically what He wants you to hear and put into practice. It is good to continue learning and growing throughout life. Be interested in the experiences of others. Learn from them. Ask God to help you see your life and experience in the greater context of what He is doing in the world around you. Remember it's not all about you.

2. Keep your expectations realistic while exercising bold faith. God is pleased when you take steps of faith. Develop new skills and significant personal growth which will require you to exercise bold faith. The connection between expectations and stress is very real. Sometimes stress reactions are intensified because of unrealistic expectations. They can also set you up for failure and discouragement. You need wisdom to navigate the minefield that lies between bold faith and realistic expectations. Ask God for wisdom and discernment.

3. Maintain a balanced life. Life is often about finding and maintaining balance. Stress has a way of pushing you out of balance; you can get tunnel vision and not see simple or obvious solutions. You can become out of balance with either too much or too little stimulation. The physical body begins to demand attention, attempting to force us back to what has been called homeostasis (another word for balance). Sometimes the most helpful steps are taking time to catch your breath, relax a bit, take stock of what is truly important and reorganize life around your strategic priorities. It is important to remember the powerful role of simple things like eating a healthy diet, getting enough rest and proper physical exercise.

4. Establish and maintain a healthy support system. During times of stress you need the emotional support of others. Sometimes your stress reactions cause you to push others away. You can distance yourself from the very people you need most. It is vital to understand how to establish and maintain a healthy support network.

5. Make sure that Jesus Christ is Lord over every area of your life. God often uses stress and distress to draw our attention to areas of life that need spiritual attention. The desire to live a God-centered life will be challenged by everyday events. The real battleground is over who is in charge and how we respond.

6. Relate to God in light of His perfections. The experiences of stress and distress call you to evaluate your behavior and relate to God in light of His perfections. This makes God-centered living practical and intensely meaningful. We are called to reflect (in a limited way) God's perfections to a watching world.

7. Spend time alone with God in prayer and the study of His word. Ultimately life is about relationships. Your relationship with God grows more intimate as you spend time alone with Him in prayer and reflective study of the Bible.

#4
Theological Foundation–The Perfections Of God

God-centered living begins with clear God-centered thinking. Most people assume that they know the essentials about God. Yet, they would have a hard time answering the question, "Who is this God that you worship?" This is why I wrote *God Talk: 13 Things Everybody Needs To Know About God*. It lays out a simple method, using memory hooks, to help the average person understand and remember a basic outline on this subject. It equips laymen to speak boldly and more effectively about God.

Knowing, delighting in and celebrating who God is, is at the core of successful living. It is the basis for all God-centered living. It provides purpose for life and answers to your deepest questions. When you lose sight of God in daily life you pay a terrible price and often experience great distress. Abundant life is found in knowing God and keeping Him at the center of all that you do. In order to know Him you must know about Him. It is in the Scriptures and through the incarnation of His Son Jesus Christ that we learn about God (Hebrews 1:1-2).

The term "the perfections of God" refers to the attributes of God.[1] Or simply put, what God is like.

Charles C. Ryrie in his *Basic Theology* devotes Chapter Six to "The Perfections of God." He discusses how the attributes of God are generally classified into categories such as natural and moral, absolute and relative, and incommunicable and communicable. He then proceeds to assemble a catalog of fourteen perfections of God. His list includes: eternity, absolute and relative, and incommunicable and communicable.[2] He then proceeds to assemble a catalog of fourteen perfections of God. His list includes: eternity, freedom, immutability, infinity, holiness, love, omnipotence, omnipresence, omniscience, righteousness, simplicity, sovereignty, truth and unity.[3]

---

[1] *J. I. Packer, Knowing God (Downers Grove, IL: IV Press, 1973), p. 16.*
[2] *According to Ryrie, God's non-moral or natural attributes "like his self-existence and infinity, belong to the constitution of God" and the moral attributes are qualities "like justice and holiness." "Absolute attributes include those which belong to the essence of God as considered in itself (eternity, infinity), and relative attributes belong to the essence of God as considered in relation to His creation (like omniscience)." Incommunicable attributes "are those which belong only to God (eternity, infinity), while [communicable] are those which are found in a relative or limited degree in people (wisdom, justice)." Charles C. Ryrie, Basic Theology (Wheaton: Victor Books, 1987), p. 36.*
[3] *Ibid., pp. 36-44.*

There is no single all-inclusive list of God's attributes. Although there is general agreement and great similarity among the lists, it is easy to get lost among the trees and lose perspective on this important subject. Most of us need help when it comes to remembering the specifics regarding the attributes of God. I have found that a practical way to think about this complex subject is to group them into five clusters. This makes the attributes easier to remember and aids me in celebrating and delighting in who God is and integrating the implication of that truth into daily life.

The five clusters of the perfections of God are:

1. ***Sovereignty***
2. ***Righteousness***
3. ***Love***
4. ***Truth***
5. ***Grace***

You have most likely noticed that these five clusters of the attributes of God correspond to the five principles in Section One that are the biblical answer to the personal side of managing stress. 1. Sovereignty and control is both how stress gets started but also the solution as we come to understand and practice God's sovereignty over everyday events. Numbers 2-4 provide our basis for a strategy for managing emotions using the Head – Heart – Hands model and relate them to Truth, Love, and Righteousness. And of course, number 5, Grace corresponds to our identity in Christ as contrasted with the ladder way of thinking. I have also used the memory hook of the fingers of the hand to help people remember these truths as is shared in the *God Talk* book.

#5
What is Stress and How Does it Work?

Most people say that they know what stress is, yet if asked to give a definition, hesitate and find precise wording difficult. Even in academic circles we find this to be true. Fran White wrote a few years ago, "There is a general lack of agreement on the definition of stress."[4] "Selye, the endocrinologist who introduced the concept of stress as a research topic, limited its meaning to nonspecific bodily responses to any demand. He called the entire physical process the general adaptation syndrome."[5] Hans Selye is often quoted because he was first to coin the term *stress* but I find his definition rather unhelpful to most people.

Thomas Holmes is frequently quoted in articles about stress. He published the "Social Readjustment Rating Scale" which attempted to measure stress in terms of units of change that had taken place in a person's life within a year.[6] This is helpful because it reminds us that it is real-life events like the death of a spouse or being fired from a job that cause stress, however I find his attempt to put numbers to these events a bit arbitrary. More helpful to me is this description. "It is other people and events out in the environment we must relate to that set off the stress response."[7] Or as Ken Williams said, "Stress is our personal response to any events which require adaptation on the part of the total person."[8]

I have used this definition, "Stress is a person's reaction to the demands placed upon him by circumstantial events. Simply put, stress is a response to what happens."[9]

---

[4] *David G. Benner, ed. Baker Encyclopedia of Psychology, (Grand Rapids: Baker Book House, 1985), p. 1121.*

[5] *Ibid. p. 1121.*

[6] *Paul D. Meier, Frank B. Minirth, Frank Wichern, Introduction to Psychology and Counseling, (Grand Rapids: Baker Book House, 1982), pp. 261-3.*

[7] *John D. Adams, ed. Understanding and Managing Stress, (San Diego: University Associates Inc.,1980), p. 11.*

[8] *Ken Williams, "Biblical Strategies for Handling Stress" Unpublished paper, Wycliffe Bible Translators.*

[9] *Lee Hotchkiss, Handling Stress Effectively. (Secunderabad, India: OM Authentic Books, 2007), p. 22.*

So far we have seen that stress is our response to an event (called a stressor). Now let's think about how stress works. My favorite study on stress was done on 94 air traffic controllers at O'Hare, at that time the world's busiest airport. It found that only two controllers stayed more than ten years, two- thirds had ulcers or symptoms of ulcers, 35 had been removed for psychiatric reasons and the incidence of high blood pressure was four times that of pilots. It stated, "They often felt they were not in control...[10] That is not a very comforting thought when you fly in and out of busy airports.

The O'Hare study illustrates what other researchers have found. Seligman (1975), "demonstrates clearly...that distress and depression are generated when a subject does not have control over his environment[11] and "85% of significant depressions are precipitated by specific life stresses.[12]

Stress is really about control. You experience stress when something happens that does not match your expectations of what is ideal. It is about power (or lack of it) to make things happen according to your agenda. Put in fancier language, "The experience of little or no rewarding interaction with the environment causes the person to feel sad and blue. The key notion is that being depressed results from too few person-environment interactions with positive outcomes for the person."[13]

Why do different people react differently to the same event? Why is there such a wide range of stress reactions? Daniel Goldman's answer is, "Events are what one makes of them. How one construes events determines whether or not they will be stressful." And, "Stress, (according to a model developed by Richard Lazarus) occurs when the demands of the environment in a person's eyes exceed his resources."[15]

---

[10] *Keith W. Sehnert, Stress/Unstress, (Minneapolis: Augsburg Publishing House, 1981), p. 41.*
[11] *Adams p. 1121.*
[12] *Meier, Minirth, Wichern, p. 167.*
[13] *Lewinsohn, Sullivan and Grosscup, "Changing reinforcing events: An approach to the treatment of depression" (Psychotherapy: Theory, Research and Practice, 1980), p. 324.*
[14] *Daniel Goleman, Vital Lies, Simple Truths, (New York: Simon and Schuster, 1985), p. 47.*

#6

Digging Deeper into The Physiology of Stress and Overall Health

If you are struggling with stress and its long-term effects on your health as I do, I would suggest that you start by doing your own research. Be careful who you listen to. We are exposed to a great deal of misinformation and propaganda - much of it motivated by financial interests. Ask God for discernment. Sorting out what is worthwhile and what is not takes real wisdom. I am reminded by three New Testament texts that instruct us to be cautious when it comes to thinking about food (Mark 7:18-19; 1 Timothy 4:1-5; Hebrews 13:9). As God has been eliminated from most of the public discussion of health and wellness we can see that medical science, diet and exercise has become a new replacement religion.

I will list below some of the doctors I have found helpful. They are speaking out to inform and interpret some of the new research findings. Most have spent years in clinical practice and speak to results that they have seen firsthand. They are people who seem to be willing to go against the flow and explore better ways of viewing and treating disease. They tend to fall under the category of what is called functional medicine. That means they promote a personalized approach, listen to the individual and search for the underlying cause. Too often busy doctors make a quick diagnosis and write a prescription without taking the time to evaluate the important role that stress may be playing. I have been fascinated to see a renewed interest in the complexity of the systems of the human body. Another area of recent interest and growing agreement among the medical community is that of the important role of the micro biome. This does appears to be a very promising new frontier in medicine. The knowledge base in medical science is constantly changing and increasing. What science calls fact one day is often dismissed as error the next.

The following list of doctors can be easily found on YouTube by searching for them by name. I am not endorsing them but I have found their podcasts, interviews and lectures informative. One of my disappointments is that most of these and others in the bio-science field hold to an evolutionary worldview. As I discover more about God's creation I marvel at His design (Psalm 139:13-16). May God give you wisdom and discernment to determine what has value and what to reject.

Dr. Daniel Amen, MD Psychiatrist *(He is a pioneer in using imaging in brain health and has performed over 40,000 brain scans).*

Dr. Dale Bredesen, MD *Neurologist (He shares conclusions gleaned from decades of work in the laboratory and clinical practice specializing in brain health and Alzheimer's. He is best known for his two books, The End of Alzheimer's and The End of Alzheimer's Program).*

Dr. Annette Bosworth, MD *Internal Medicine (She is in clinical practice and published a good beginner's guide for understanding ketogenic diet and also tells the story of her mother's cancer journey in her book, Anyway You Can, 2018).*

Dr. William Davis, MD *Cardiologist and author of numerous books including Wheat Belly and Super Gut).*

Dr. Sten Ekberg, Holistic Medicine *(He is a prolific podcast presenter and a good educator for laymen with solid material with easy-to-understand explanations on nutrition and health issues).*

Dr. Steven R. Gundry, MD *Cardiologist and Heart Surgeon (He has done 10,000 heart surgeries, has written several books on plant-based diet, aging, how cells work and leaky gut. Two of his excellent books include The Plant Paradox and The Longevity Paradox, 2019).*

Dr. Mark Hyman, MD *Functional Medicine (He has extensive clinical practice and is a well-known leader in the functional medicine movement).*

Dr. Todd Lepine, MD *Internal Medicine (His clinical practice specializes in Integrative Functional Medicine).*

Dr. William Li, MD *(He is a world-renowned physician, scientist, speaker, and author of Eat to Beat Disease).*

Dr. Robert H. Lustig, MD, MSL *Neuroendrocrinologist (Author and lecturer, speaks eloquently about the dangers of processed foods, most recent book, Metabolical, 2022).*

Dr. David Perlmutter, MD *Neurologist (Specializing in preventative medicine and nutrition he is the author of two groundbreaking books, Brain Maker, and The Grain Brain Whole Life Plan).*

Made in the USA
Columbia, SC
22 May 2024

35601279R00070